easyJet Rising

Tony Anderson

This cover has been designed using resources from Freepik.com

This book is published by
Oranssi Publishing

A CIP record for this book
is available from the British Library

ISBN 978-1-9162645-1-9

Dedication

To British Airways - your high fares made this book possible

Contents

Chapter One

A free lunch

April 1995: My involvement with the low-cost airline easyJet and its billionaire founder began with an early morning phone call from a London head hunter. I vaguely remembered an e-mail setting the conversation up, but surely not for 7am? Sensing I wasn't yet fully awake, she cut swiftly to the chase. A start-up airline, with strong financial backing, was seeking a marketing director to mastermind its launch. The man behind the new venture was a young Greek Cypriot entrepreneur called Stelios Haji-Ioannou. I could tell she had been practising the pronunciation by the way the surname rolled easily off her tongue.

'He's an impressive guy, definitely worth meeting,' she said.

There was silence as I fought back a temptation to claim I'd heard of him.

'Can you make lunch next week?' she added.

Another pause. I was still half-asleep, like a dinosaur that's been given a sharp kick in the rear end, it had taken a while for the information to reach my brain. I replied in the affirmative.

A cold shower, immediately followed by a hot coffee had the required invigorating effect. Suddenly my mind was buzzing. Whoever this Stelios dude was, I needed to know more about him, and fast. Information gathering back then was firmly in the Stone Age: no publically available internet and consequently no Google search at your fingertips. A trip to the local library unearthed a few precious nuggets of information. My lunch appointment was a twenty-eight-year-old graduate of the London School of Economics; he'd already set up a successful shipping company of his own and the Haji-Ioannou family were fabulously wealthy. I wrote these points down in my notebook, underlining the last one twice for good measure. Backers with deep pockets are an essential pre-requisite for any aviation start-up.

This wasn't your typical recruitment process. There was no battery of mathematical or verbal reasoning tests to overcome, no personality questionnaire or psychological profiling. Instead, my prospects of landing the easyJet job hinged on a sixty-minute lunch meeting with the airline's founder. Figuring punctuality wouldn't win it, but that lateness might cost me my chance, I arrived early. Stelios was already seated at our table. He stood up to shake my hand and I sized him up. He was a well-built man of southern Mediterranean appearance, curly dark hair and broad shoulders; casually dressed, visibly relaxed but with a glint in his eyes that told you he meant business. His English was grammatically impeccable, though a distinctive accent betrayed the fact he'd been born and brought up in Greece.

After a brief exchange of pleasantries, we sat down. Food was the last thing on my mind. I scanned the menu in a nanosecond and ordered the salmon ravioli: a sensible choice if you want to put the act of eating onto autopilot. Then, without further ado, my interrogation began. Stelios was direct, incisive and pretty much relentless. He unleashed a barrage of questions, general ones at first – family, school, university – then focused in detail on my previous employment with British Airways and Thomas Cook. He told me these two companies would be amongst his biggest enemies. When I described myself as a potential 'gamekeeper turned poacher', he seemed to find this highly amusing. A plate of steaming ravioli appeared out of nowhere. Stelios nodded at me to eat up; it was his turn to do the talking. 'Let me tell you what I'm going to do,' he said.

Without breaking eye contact, I took a forkful of pasta and listened as my inquisitor outlined his plans for 'Project easyJet'. It was a bold and audacious vision. The future he painted for the proposed airline was fraught with risk, but utterly compelling. Stelios was a born storyteller who exuded confidence and self-belief. He explained how the aviation industry was on the brink of massive change. The catalyst was the ongoing process of European deregulation. Long standing agreements, obscure rules and arcane regulations were being torn up, removing barriers to new entrants and enabling truly price-led competition. National airlines had treated the continent's travellers as cash cows and had been milking them for decades. Stelios, was on a one-man mission to kick down the door to the dairy. Currently that door was double locked, barred and bolted. Opening it would require considerable financial firepower, but as I kept reminding myself, the Haji-Ioannous were well and truly loaded.

He paused briefly before moving on to the subject of brands and branding. Stelios was a marketer by instinct rather than training, but he knew his stuff. Launching an airline was in his view a great way to build a brand. Incredibly, his aspirations extended far beyond the aviation sector. The eventual goal was to develop a family of brands under the 'easy' umbrella. But first things first; making the airline a commercial success and establishing easyJet as a household name would create the platform needed to realise his longer-term ambitions.

By now Stelios had been talking for some time and had moved on from the big picture to the detail. I've never been a creature of detail. While easyJet's founder rattled through various aspects of the airline's financial model citing load factors, route pricing and cost of customer acquisition, my mind wandered for a moment. I mulled over in my head how much his family was actually worth; might it be as much a billion dollars? How many planes did that buy you these days anyway? Perhaps sensing a loss of concentration on my part, Stelios stopped talking and fixed me with a basilisk-like stare.

'What do you think?' he asked.

Oh shit, I thought. The question had caught me completely off-guard. I had no idea what he'd just been saying.

'I think you're completely crazy but count me in,' I ad-libbed.

There was silence; tumbleweed blew through the room. I grinned nervously, hoping for a smile in return, but his face was utterly impassive. Abruptly, Stelios stood up. Our meeting was over and we shook hands. Had I blown my chance with a few ill-chosen words? It was impossible to tell.

The head hunter had told me to expect an answer by the end of the week. Instead the phone call came midway through my drive home to Peterborough. The job was mine if I wanted it. Two minutes later I turned the car around and headed straight back to London. I'd just become easyJet's third employee.

It is a truth universally acknowledged that anyone leaving a well-paid corporate job for an airline start-up needs their head examined. My boss was a director of Thomas Cook and a cigar-chomping industry veteran. Evidently more used to firing people than having them walk out on him, he shook his head disparagingly as I handed in my notice.

'You won't get a pay-off when they go bust.'

It was a fair comment. Notwithstanding its enduring allure, civil aviation was famously and fabulously unprofitable. When the shit hit the turbofan, redundant employees invariably found themselves last in a long line of creditors. Most walked away with nothing but an addiction to the smell of kerosene and stories of adventures in foreign lands to share with their grandchildren.

If it was tough to survive as an established operator, it was even tougher for the new kids on the block. The failure rate among start-up airlines within the first two years of operation ran close to 90%. Hardly surprising, then, that the announcement of easyJet's arrival was greeted with scorn and derision by the industry establishment. 'Europe isn't ready for the peanut airline,' sneered a British Airways spokesman quoted by *The Times* newspaper in the days leading up to our launch.

Yet I was going into this adventure with my eyes open, having first encountered the low-cost airline phenomenon four years earlier while working for BA on a secondment to their New York marketing office. The United States was where it had all began. Deregulation of civil aviation back in the 1970s had spawned a wave of start-ups including Southwest the 'Daddy' of low-cost airlines. This didn't just trigger a price war, but led to an industry shake-out that was almost Darwinian in its harshness. Many of the new carriers folded, but amidst the financial carnage the alchemists of Southwest had found a formula that worked. Under the inspired leadership of legendary chief executive, Herb Kelleher, the Dallas-based airline delivered a tidy profit year after year in an industry awash with red ink. Southwest was credited with breaking an effective oligopoly of the big American carriers and changing the face of the industry. As an employee of British Airways I enjoyed discounted fares with other carriers, but was amazed to find Southwest's regular prices were often lower than I could get through the BA staff travel programme. I returned to the UK, convinced the no-frills concept would one day come to Europe. Now, out of the blue, a chance to be part of the low-cost revolution had landed in my lap.

I relished the opportunity to cross swords with my former employer. After completing the British Airways graduate training programme in the late 80s, I'd joined their marketing distribution department as part of a small team seeking to develop direct sales. There had been much to learn in my aviation apprenticeship with 'the dark side', but I remember it first and foremost as a time of frustration and missed opportunity. BA employed a lot of bright people, but while innovation often sparked it rarely flared. The airline was weighed down by its history, cultural baggage and aversion to commercial risk. Somewhere deep in the core of the company was an innate conservatism that stifled truly progressive thinking.

I couldn't see myself making a long-term career with British Airways, but the flight benefits made it hard to say goodbye. Then fate took a hand. A chance meeting with Peter Middleton, the chief executive of Thomas Cook, in the autumn of 1990, led to a job offer and I threw in the towel. The next four years I spent away from the front lines of aviation, coming up with new product ideas for the travel giant. Now I was leaving secure employment with one of the longest established and best known travel brands in the world, to join an unknown start-up led by a twenty-eight-year-old industry novice that had yet to fly a single passenger. How did it feel? It felt utterly exhilarating. I was back in the airline business and absolutely up for the fight of a lifetime.

Chapter Two

Man with a plan

The first rule when starting a business of any size is to have a plan: its importance makes it worth repeating and underlining: 'Have a Plan'. You can change it, rip it up in frustration and – in future years – look back and laugh at how off the mark it was; however, you need to *have a plan.* According to the late US president and five-star general, Dwight Eisenhower, no battle plan survives more than five minutes' contact with the enemy, but he still cited the need to 'HAVE A PLAN'.

The earliest version of the easyJet business plan I saw had been printed on a wad of A4 paper. My copy was stamped *confidential.* As soon as my background and references had been checked, I was allowed to take it home, sealed in a manila envelope.

The packet had been handed to me by Nick Manoudakis, the airline's finance director. Nick was a craggy-faced, chain-smoking graduate of the prestigious University of Berkeley, California. Greek by birth, he had personal connections to the

Haji-Ioannou family. For many months prior to my arrival, easyJet's chief bean counter had been working alongside Stelios putting together the business plan now entrusted to my care. Nick stressed that the precious document could not be allowed to fall into the hands of British Airways. I was well aware of BA's reputation for corporate skulduggery earned in highly publicised battles with Laker Airways and Virgin Atlantic. Best not take any chances. The safest thing to do would be to read it when I got home.

With the envelope zipped securely in my rucksack, I boarded the Piccadilly line to King's Cross. It took just a couple of minutes before curiosity got the better of me. Surely there could be no harm in taking a quick peek? I unzipped my bag and stealthily removed the confidential contents. At that precise moment a sixth sense prompted me to look up. My instincts were spot on: I was being watched. From the other side of the carriage a sinister-looking, thin-faced man sporting a distinctive Chicago Bears beanie hat fixed me with an unwavering stare. Come to think of it, he'd followed me on to the train at Green Park station. Paranoia set in. Could 'Mr Beanie Hat' be a British Airways spy? I put the envelope down, doing my best to look nonchalant.

Within five seconds of disembarking at King's Cross, I realised, to my horror, the plan was still lying on the seat. I lunged desperately at the closing doors only for them to slam shut just inches from my outstretched hands. 'For fuck's sake!' I mouthed silently while hammering on the compartment door to no avail. The train pulled away and my short-lived easyJet career flashed before me in an instant. It was a complete and unmitigated disaster.

Somehow I bluffed and blustered my way through the next few days. Trust me, it's hard giving credible answers to questions about a business plan you haven't read. Finally, an opportunity presented itself. In a carefully choreographed manoeuvre, while Nick disappeared for a cigarette break, I ran his copy of the plan through a nearby photocopier. With a freshly printed facsimile of the confidential document in my possession I went home, locked the door, poured myself a cold beer and read it from cover to cover.

The draft easyJet business plan read like a Haynes manual to starting a low-cost airline. A logical step-by-step approach, written in punchy prose, illustrated with neat tables of numbers and mini route maps. It was the sort of sweet-talking document penned by sharp-suited, silver-tongued management consultants that suckers in the unseasoned investor. Setting up a new airline? Simply follow the instructions. How could it possibly go wrong?

The plan drew heavily on the tried-and-tested business models of North American low-cost carriers, most notably the Georgia-based Valujet and Southwest Airlines, which had its headquarters in Dallas, Texas. The first step was to establish easyJet on the key routes between the UK capital and Scotland. Initial frequency was set at three flights a day. Morning and evening timings were carefully chosen to capture the business person making a day trip. Many of these travellers either worked for, or were visiting, small- and medium-sized businesses in Luton and the surrounding area. They had little or no loyalty to British Airways who had been robbing them blind for years.

Scotland was just a staging post in the business plan. The next step would be expansion into continental Europe, concentrating on high-traffic routes where easyJet could grow the market. Some of the more obvious candidate cities were on the initial hit list: Madrid and Rome for the volume; Nice and Geneva for the growth potential. No surprises there. On the other hand, I harboured doubts about the inclusion of Oslo and Stockholm. Airfares on both routes were undeniably high but they were relatively small population centres lacking the lure of sun, sea and sangria.

The section on pricing was a breath of fresh air. In comparison to the complex tariffs operated by conventional airlines, easyJet's pricing structure was simplicity itself. The plan envisaged a small number of bands ranging from £29 to £59 one way on the Scottish routes and up to £99 outside the UK. Nick was adamant that £29 was to be our absolute lowest fare on any route. Breaching it would be the airline equivalent of crossing the Rubicon. Anything set below that level, he insisted, would make it impossible for easyJet (or any other carrier) to make money. I remember nodding in agreement with Nick's words of wisdom. At that point, had someone told me that within a decade low-cost carriers would not only be flying tens of millions of passengers at fares as low as 99p, and they would also be among the most profitable airlines in history, I would have dismissed them out of hand.

The business plan anticipated a return on investment of some forty per cent by the end of the second year. It was the triumph of hope over decades of aviation experience. I kept reminding myself of easyJet's ownership and access to capital. The important thing was to demonstrate the long-term viability of the business model, rather than to maximise profitability in the early years of operation. At the plan's heart was the most fundamental fallacy of all: a belief that our fate hinged on persuading people to fly for the first time. In retrospect, while new flyers made an important contribution to growth, a far more significant driver was easyJet's ability to get people who already flew to fly more.

Financial discipline was firmly enshrined in the plan, and rightly so: many start-up airlines fail because they simply run out of money to pay the bills. Life as an airline is all about managing cash. The bills for fuel, air-traffic control and airport charges (not to mention wages) are unceasing, even in the depths of winter when passengers are less inclined to fly. Ever wary of the possibility of airlines going bust, airports, fuel companies and other key suppliers are unforgiving in their management of debtors. If this new venture was going to have a fighting chance, it would need cash – and lots of it. Fortunately, the young man behind the venture had money: an initial five million pounds borrowed from his father to start the airline, and access to more if – or more like it when, he needed it. But easyJet was to be no rich kid's plaything. Stelios was determined that the airline would have a ruthless approach to cost management. From day one, no-frills was to mean exactly that.

The choice of aircraft was a hugely significant decision. The business plan suggested easyJet would operate the McDonnell Douglas DC9-30, the equipment of choice for Valujet. In the second-hand market they could be picked up for around $5.5m apiece. After some deliberation, and with a nod to Southwest Airlines, Stelios opted instead for Boeing. It was almost certainly the right call. We started the airline with two leased 737s, the workhorse for North American budget airlines in the early 90s. Ours were the 737-200 version, configured to carry 130 passengers at a seat pitch of 29 inches. This compared with the 115 passengers and 32 inch seat pitch configuration characteristic of competitors flying the same model. By the standards of today's gleaming low-cost fleets, the aircraft were long in the tooth. But they were relatively fuel efficient, reasonably modern jets. Our two were coming out of service with the Brussels based airline *Virgin Express*, which was in the process of upgrading to the more modern 737-300 variant.

The first time I saw the aircraft they were sitting in a Luton airport maintenance hangar, surrounded by scaffolding and waiting to be painted. From a distance they looked in good shape but viewed up close it was apparent the previous owners had worked them hard. The cabin windows bore scratches and the catering trollies were dented. If you looked closely enough, you could see that the carpets were fraying and stained in places.

Vestiges of Virgin's distinctive crimson branding could be spotted everywhere. The logos on the galleys and trolleys were easily covered up with orange easyJet stickers but on a sunny day you could still make out faint traces of the tell-tale red lettering underneath the freshly painted hull. It wasn't the time for nit-picking or buyer's remorse. When Stelios announced he'd signed the aircraft leasing agreement, a cheer went up around the office. It was a major milestone and a moment to savour: we were no longer a virtual airline, easyJet had secured its first two planes and things were about to get serious.

Chapter Three

Stansted versus Luton

My automatic assumption was that our new airline would be based at Stansted. It seemed a natural choice at the time, especially for Nick (he'd already found a house within easy commuting distance of the Essex airport!). By this point, we'd been through several rounds of civilised negotiations with tea served on bone china cups at the British Airports Authority Stansted offices. It felt to me like they were going through the motions. The deal on the table was far from compelling and the airport management was utterly intransigent.

In an attempt to break the negotiating impasse, Stelios played the Luton card and a visit was hastily arranged. Stelios liked what he saw. Luton airport was clearly underutilised. There was virtually no scheduled traffic and its biggest customers were large charter operators like Thomson and Monarch, to whom we later subcontracted our engineering. The airport's management, led by progressive chief executive

Richard Gooding, was desperate to secure more scheduled services and was willing to cut us a deal.

As easyJet's marketing director and the man responsible for selling the virtues of our new home to potential customers, I winced when Stelios told us he'd come to a decision and it wasn't Stansted. What the hell was he thinking; surely he couldn't be serious? Luton was all about package holidays. The Bedfordshire airport served as the departure point for millions of holidaymakers travelling on charter flights to Spain, Portugal and other Mediterranean destinations. The mere mention of Luton conjured up images of flip-flops, straw donkeys and tasteless souvenirs constructed from glued-together sea shells. I returned home that evening feeling downcast but not despondent; I had faith in Stelios's judgement but the choice of airport for his new airline felt like a self-inflicted wound.

I got up the next day in a more positive frame of mind. Perhaps I was placing too much store by my own opinions; what did others think of Luton? In the minds of the British public the airport was still associated with the actress and model Lorraine Chase. She had been the star of an infamous television advertising campaign for the drinks brand *Campari* back in the 80s. To gain a better understanding of the airport's history, Stelios and I met Lorraine for tea at the stuffy Hurlingham polo club in Putney, London. Walking through the grand entrance of the Georgian clubhouse was like going back in time to

Dickensian London. Had British Airways been around in Victorian times, its executives would doubtless have met at the Hurlingham to complain about the quality of port, the price of imported cigars and the insolence of chimney sweeps. There was a minor delay at the club's entrance when an officious doorman insisted we put on ties before being let in. Lorraine was charming but I didn't learn anything from the meeting, except perhaps that combining a striped shirt with spotted neckwear is not a good look.

What could Luton offer passengers besides fading memories of a one-time minor celebrity? Quite a lot as it happens, but towards the top of the list was a four letter word: time. Most people correctly assumed the Bedfordshire airport to be cheaper than its London alternatives, but less immediately apparent was the punctuality factor. You didn't need to be a rocket scientist to work it out. There were significantly fewer flights and the vast majority were short-haul rather than intercontinental. This conferred an automatic time-keeping advantage on a Luton-based airline compared with a competitor operating out of congested Heathrow.

The announcement in July 1995 that easyJet would indeed base itself at Luton was met first by scepticism and then with shrugs of acceptance by my travel industry friends. In their eyes the decision would have no bearing on the inevitable outcome; the sole barometer of success was the length of time before the airline passed into bankruptcy. At best we'd made a tactical move that bought another six months of survival. We would avoid head-to-head competition at the airport itself and could grow modestly by appealing to travellers in the Luton catchment area. But the sceptics had missed the point. We weren't setting out to be a niche airline with the sole aim of survival. Stelios was thinking bigger, much bigger.

There was no doubt about it: the man had *cojones.* This was especially true when it came to his radical ideas on getting the product to market. At that time, airlines typically sold only a small proportion of their seats direct to the public, mainly over the telephone or through airport ticket offices. The balance was sold through travel agents, either of the business or high street variety. The agents exerted a vice-like grip on the distribution chain. It was larceny on a grand scale. Scheduled flights were an absurdly simple product to sell and there was limited opportunity for a middleman to add value. Despite this, the agents were typically paid between ten and fifteen per cent of the ticket price. Their earnings could be further boosted by over-ride payments and bonus deals. While travel agents gorged on a fat slice of pie, the airlines were left to fight over the crumbs. Carriers were paying more in commissions than they were on their fuel bills. It simply couldn't carry on. If history tells us anything it is that all things too good to be true eventually come to an end. So it proved for the majority of high street travel agents. They had been swimming naked for years and the tide was about to go out on them.

Selling direct was a simple and bold decision. Ours would be the first airline anywhere in the world to completely cut out the middleman. The move put clear-blue water between easyJet and every other carrier on the planet. But it wasn't a total shot in the dark: key trends were working in our favour. Not only did the UK have the world's second-highest penetration of credit cards per capita, but there was an established culture of buying over the telephone, with the likes of First Direct Bank and Direct Line insurance having blazed a trail for us to follow. From the day of my arrival at easyJet, I'd argued the direct sell case vehemently. Fundamentally, it was a huge gamble. We were banking on the long-term costs of building and sustaining a brand through advertising being lower than agent commissions and associated costs.

Attention turned to the details of the marketing plan and how we would get the message across. Our target market was defined as people who paid the fares out of their own pocket. This audience embraced a broad range of sub-groups: switchers from road and rail; owners of holiday homes; as well as small- and medium-sized businesses. In short, pretty much everyone aside from those travelling on business with the largest and most profligate companies. To reach this target audience of many millions, the marketing budget made available to me was the princely sum of £400,000. It was a fraction of what I had anticipated and believed to be necessary. Initially I thought the budget was a joke; then, when I'd recovered, I viewed it as a challenge. Large-scale campaigns of the kind envisaged when I first joined easyJet were out of the question. What's more, on that kind of money, full-service advertising agencies were also ruled out. To make the numbers work, we'd rely heavily on self-generated PR and homemade, low-cost ads in the classified sections of newspapers.

Somewhat incongruously I'd spent my first six weeks working for my new employer, based in a swanky townhouse on Curzon Street in the heart of Mayfair. By then we were a fledgling team of four plus Stelios. We shared the building with the UK-based staff of Stelmar, our owner's up-market shipping company. It was an unlikely and uneasy co-habitation. We were regarded with sympathetic curiosity, like mice destined for a particularly unpleasant laboratory experiment. A laminated sign taped to the wall above a photocopier declared in large bold type 'not for use by eazyjet employees'. The coffee jars in the cupboard and milk in the shared fridge had 'Stelmar only' written on the side with a marker pen. An expensive-looking tin of individually foil wrapped chocolate biscuits from Fortnum & Mason, previously on open display in the kitchen, was hidden away in a desk drawer.

The start-up team occupied a separate upper floor of the building, isolated from the shipping staff and any potential visitors. It was as if we were a mad aunt or other embarrassing elderly relative kept upstairs so as not to embarrass the occupants in front of their guests.

We got out before things turned nasty. Luton airport made us an offer and the easyJet team moved out of Curzon Street overnight. I shook the dust off my feet on the way out. Mayfair was no place to base a low-cost airline and Stelios knew it.

Chapter Four

Welcome to easyLand

Any illusions I might have harboured about the quality of our new working environment were quickly dispelled on arrival at Luton. The contrast with the opulence of Mayfair was dramatic – picture a large, open-plan working space with paint peeling from the walls inside a corrugated tin shack smelling of damp. The sound of aircraft arriving and departing from the adjacent runway was clearly audible. Luton Airport had generously thrown in our office accommodation to sweeten the deal.

Our new home was unfurnished. Nick and I assembled a set of grey functional steel desks purchased as a job lot from an office supply shop. There were eight of them and it took a decent chunk out of our first morning. There then came a moment that might have been lifted from one of those classic Western movies starring Clint Eastwood. We surveyed the room and realised that not all desk positions were created equal. Think of it in terms of the good, the bad and the ugly. The ‘good’ position was next to the window, looking out on to the airport taxiway, an attractive enough berth provided you were wearing headphones. Pretty much every other placing bar one, fell into the ‘bad’ category. Stelios, however, was quick to choose the ‘ugly’ option. In accordance with the boss’s instructions, we placed his desk outside the door to the gents’ toilet. Indisputably the worst possible location in the room, it was the innermost circle of Dante’s inferno. On a cold day it reeked of disinfectant, while on a hot day more savoury aromas competed for your attention. The precedent having been set, other members of the start-up team felt no inclination to argue about their own seating positions.

Already there were hints that easyJet might be on to something. Dave McCulloch, a highly respected industry veteran, jumped ship from Jersey European Airways to become our operations director. I was no longer the only full-time employee with an aviation background. The new hires were coming thick and fast. You can’t run a modern airline without computers and we needed someone qualified to get the office up and running. So easyJet’s next recruit and employee number seven, was a techie. Chilled out and laid back, albeit with a questionable taste in music, his name was Trevor Noble. We poached him from the company that sold us the hardware. The first task Trevor was given on joining was to install and wire up our network. Within an hour of switching on my PC for the first time, there was a popping sound, a smell of burning and the screen went blank. Needless to say, our newly appointed trouble-shooter was nowhere to be found and calls to his phone went through to voicemail. A familiar scenario to anyone who's ever relied on support provided by an unresponsive IT helpdesk. It was another sign that easyJet had become a proper company.

The premises hadn't been chosen on the basis of comfort or architectural merit, and a polite description would be 'aesthetically challenged'. It might have been a serious contender for the title of Britain's ugliest building, inside and out. Stelios appeared oblivious. We gave the place a deep clean, bought a couple of pot plants from the garden centre and at the earliest opportunity called in the painters. It was a modest step forward, a bit like putting lipstick on a pig. The smell of fresh paint hung in the air for weeks, crowding out the whiff of damp, on hot days the faint aroma of urine drifted through the room. Provided you shut your eyes, wore headphones and put a tent peg on your nose it was a tolerable enough working environment.

Meanwhile, forty miles away to the West of London (though it felt more like a small planet on the spiral arm of a distant galaxy), construction was underway on 'Waterside' a new state-of-the-art corporate headquarters for arch rival British Airways. The building included six sections backing onto a 175-metre glazed atrium street; each section had a different theme based on the particular continent it represented. For instance, cherry trees were planted in the Asia-themed section and eucalyptus trees featured in the Australia-themed one. The street was paved in granite slabs and cobblestones and had bridges overhead that linked the individual buildings. Leading off the bridges were balconies that overlooked the street. The complex housed a health centre, a hairdressing salon, and a Waitrose (of course) supermarket. It was said that the design of Waterside was intended to 'both facilitate a change in the way BA staff behave at work and to support a more customer-led culture'. I saw things differently. To my eyes it was a £200m, gilt-edged, middle fingered salute to British Airway's long-suffering shareholders. The chief executive might as well have dropped his trousers and mooned at the company's annual general meeting.

A former colleague at BA had sent me through some artist's impressions of the planned new offices at Waterside with the scrawled comment 'wish you were here?' For an idea of how it made me feel, picture a shivering, famished Victorian street urchin peering through the snow-frosted window of a London townhouse to see a fire burning in the hearth, presents round the tree and a table stacked high with Christmas fare. Not for the first time I questioned my decision to join a low-cost start-up. Part of me still longed for the comfort and corporate certainty of my old employer.

I consoled myself with the thought that the millions British Airways were spending on Waterside meant less financial ammunition available for the ongoing battle with easyJet. Banishing wistful thinking from my mind, I laughed the pictures off and shared them with the team. To my surprise the taunting had a galvanising effect, the grumbling slowly subsided and we began to develop a grudging affection for our new home. Officially christened 'easyLand', with roof and walls painted in bright orange (what else?), the building was the first thing most passengers saw when their flights touched down on the tarmac. The airport's PR manager took me to one side and told me in hushed tones that it looked 'a bit tacky'. She may well have been right but we weren't finished yet. A flashing neon sign was commissioned and mounted above the front entrance. The sign-maker liked the idea of having an airline on his client list so it was dirt cheap. The day after installation Luton airport operations made us turn off the flashing light on the grounds it was distracting staff in the traffic control tower. First time visitors approaching the building might well have mistaken easyLand for a run-down strip club with a broken sign.

Stelios was also given permission to change the name of the road leading up to easyLand. His first choice of easyStreet was rejected by Luton Council but easyWay did, however, get approval and that's what the road has been known as to this day.

Growth at Luton came with its challenges. As the airline expanded we needed more office space. The first step was to take over the public spectator's area immediately adjacent to easyLand. There was some collateral damage. For years this annexe had been home to the airport's plane spotting community. They were an inoffensive group, made up almost entirely of middle-aged men with too much time on their hands. Several weeks following their traumatic eviction, a few individuals still lingered in the vicinity. Fashionably kitted out in bobble hats, tank tops and hand-knitted scarves, binoculars hanging round their necks, they stood shivering and disconsolate, on the grassy embankment next to easyLand. It was a pitiful sight to behold. I half expected a piece to camera from David Attenborough bemoaning the habitat loss of an endangered species.

The plane spotters had been moved on, though I felt a degree of unease at their displacement. My colleagues were more sanguine and reminded me that sentimentality was a luxury easyJet couldn't afford. It wasn't long before more space was needed. We began stacking hideous grey portakabins on top of one another in the office car park. It reminded me of one of those property makeover TV shows where the project has gone horribly wrong, but those present are too polite to say anything and pretend not to notice. When the builders had finished their work, easyLand had undergone a transformation.

Previously it was simply an ugly building. Now it was an ugly building with a junkyard for a garden. Putting aesthetics to one side, the financial logic behind the development was undeniable. Every inch of available space on the site was used. Over a twelve-year period between 1995 and 2002 the airline's annual turnover grew over twenty-fold, but its headquarters remained contained within the surrounding perimeter fence.

I accept that if you never worked there it's hard to understand, but for all its faults (and they were many) there was something about the office that just felt right. A big-shot lawyer up for the day from London described easyLand to me as a 'pug-ugly, orange shit-hole'. It was difficult to argue with his description; in fact, he was over-selling the place. We simply didn't care. The building fizzed with creative energy and a can-do spirit; it was easyJet's home, a statement of intent to a sceptical world and we loved it.

A little known fact is that the start-up airline was at one stage going to be named Stelair. This was a logical enough extension, given our founder had already set up a shipping company called Stelmar and later went on to establish a financial company called Stelinvest. However, shortly before I joined, Stelios had a change of heart. Sanity had trumped vanity. His ultimate intention was to develop a portfolio of businesses under a single over-arching brand. If he'd gone for *Stel* as the prefix instead of *easy* then things might have been very different. As it was, the name 'easyJet' was filed at Companies House on 1st March 1995 and the following month an application was made to register what was to become among the best known trademarks in UK corporate history.

The choice of orange was also down to Stelios. He flicked through palettes of colours and went for the brightest, boldest most shocking shade he could find. We did not know it at the time, but eventually easyJet's use of that particular shade of orange (Pantone 021c) would become so synonymous with the airline that easyGroup was able to successfully apply for a colour per se trade mark. Non-visual branding cues were not neglected; the airline's call-sign was to be EZY subjecting those who heard it to a homophone of 'easy'.

For any aviation start-up, there are effectively two launch dates. The most obvious is the day of the first flight, but the more commercially significant is the day your seats go on sale. The shorter the period between the two dates, the tougher the task becomes to hit sales targets. We aimed to open for business in the autumn of 1995 but as summer arrived we were racing against the clock. Missing the scheduled start date was unthinkable. Stelios upped the pace; late nights and weekend working became the norm. Big decisions were taken in quick succession: we chose a reservations system from the sinister-sounding company, *Sys Ops*, bought a telephone switch and set up a small call centre in a corner of our Luton offices.

Through the local job centre, we advertised for twenty staff to man the phones. There was no basic salary. Successful applicants were paid a commission of 80p for each seat sold and their earnings were uncapped. Many of our new recruits were young and lacked experience or formal qualifications, but all were highly enthusiastic. With the internet and broadband yet to take off, telephone calls were easyJet's lifeblood. There was no need to advertise our opening hours because the centre was to be staffed twenty-four hours a day, seven days a week, every day of the year including Christmas Day.

'I've lost the key,' Stelios was fond of saying when pressed to explain his open all-hours policy.

Some weeks later, we found the right person to run the call centre. John Macleod was an unflappable north Londoner and a fanatical Arsenal supporter. He was as tough as nails but with a heart of gold. He'd previously managed a telephone betting operation for Ladbrokes. With easyJet operating a strict no-refunds policy, we figured his experience of telling disappointed punters that they couldn't have their money back would come in handy. We were right. Our new recruit had a polite but insistent telephone manner capable of soothing the most irate of callers. From time to time, customers would show up at the door of easyLand to take their grievances a step further. On such occasions John's imposing frame and boxer's nose had the desired calming effect.

As October 1995 approached, the pace quickened further and successive pre-launch actions were ticked off our checklist. We appointed wise-cracking Allen Marking as easyJet's chief engineer, Mike Keane became chief pilot and Simon Gray joined from GB airways as the first head of cabin crew. The one-room office at easyLand was starting to become crowded. Over the course of a long hot summer, stale sweat was added to the pungent cocktail of smells emanating from the building. We lived in fear of toilet blockages, and the local plumber was placed on speed-dial.

From a personal standpoint things were looking up, I was no longer a one-person marketing department. Stelios finally gave the green light for me to recruit an assistant and with a bit of arm twisting was persuaded to release more money for our launch. The increased budget brought radio advertising within reach and, with the help of talented industry freelancers, Murray Partridge and Simon Confino, we recorded a couple of crude but effective radio spots. We even created an easyJet advertising jingle. Most of the remaining marketing budget was deployed across local press in Luton, London and Scotland. We'd placed a few modest classified ads in the travel sections of the national papers but somehow I doubted the BA marketing director was losing any sleep. After months of frenetic activity, everything was finally in place – easyJet was cleared for take-off.

Chapter Five

First flight

Luton Airport: 10th November 1995, a little after 7 a.m. on a dull, damp and utterly ordinary late-autumn morning. Droplets of rain pitter-pattered onto the gleaming white and orange hull of easyJet's inaugural flight to Glasgow. From a standing start, fifty-two tons of steel and aluminium, thirty-six miles of wiring and one hundred and thirty-five passengers and crew accelerated hard with a throaty roar down the runway before vanishing into a gloomy, cloud-glutted, slate-grey sky. On board flight EZY 121, occupying the cockpit jump-seat, was Stelios, the founder of what was now officially Britain's newest and brashest airline. I sat quietly towards the front of the cabin, nursing a hangover and silently cursing the early start.

On hand to film passengers as they boarded was a BBC documentary crew from 'The Money Programme'. As passengers go I would describe them as a pretty eclectic bunch. Among the first up the aircraft steps were a sprightly pair of elderly nuns, resplendent in freshly starched blue habits. It later transpired that the holy sisters had been in London to discuss the affairs of their order with a firm of financial advisers. They might well have been easyJet's first business passengers.

Perhaps appropriately for the first flight of a no-frills airline the journey itself was unremarkable in every way. No one on board could have imagined that they were witnessing a defining moment in European aviation history. The first of what now amounts to over three million easyJet flights with a cumulative passenger total exceeding half a billion … and counting.

This was it, the maiden journey, the culmination of many months of personal sacrifice and sustained effort. You might have expected easyJet's founder to be in celebratory mood but Stelios was curiously and uncharacteristically subdued. We had eaten dinner with friends and colleagues in Luton's Strathmore Hotel the previous night and he'd barely said a word. Shortly after take-off, he made a half-hearted announcement through the aircraft's PA system; I don't recall his exact words but few were listening and the speech fell flat. Enthusing comatose passengers on an early morning flight to Glasgow is a tough gig for anyone. The remainder of the journey passed in silence. I briefly nodded off and was awakened by an announcement from the pilot that we'd made up a ten-minute departure delay. As the aircraft made its final approach I peered through the window. A rain-lashed Scotland was every inch as dreary as the Luton we'd left behind. If the weather was a portent of things to come then our future looked ugly.

Moments later the orange liveried 737 brought a splash of colour to a distinctly monochrome Glasgow airport as tyre hit tarmac in a cloud of spray. Waiting to greet us at the bottom of the aircraft steps was a delegation of airport officials and minor local dignitaries, all clearly itching to get away. With camera crew in tow, Stelios and I were ushered by our welcoming committee toward the warm embrace of the Servisair VIP lounge. It was empty aside from a handful of British Airways business class passengers awaiting a boarding announcement for their flight to Heathrow. The lounge attendant eyed us suspiciously and the scowl on his face told us we had no right to be there dripping rainwater onto his plush carpet. As the BBC cameras rolled, we thumbed through our coverage in the Scottish morning papers. It didn't make for encouraging reading. The articles were the business equivalent of an obituary. On the plus side, easyJet's arrival on the Anglo-Scottish routes was welcomed, British Airway's high prices were castigated and the lack of serious competition bemoaned. But the orange airline's early demise was seen as inevitable, a temporary blip before normal service was resumed.

We were in no mood to hang around kicking our heels in Glasgow. From the moment the flight landed, I was itching to get back to the sales action at easyLand. Thankfully the thirty-minute process of cleaning and checking the aircraft passed quickly. The lounge attendant forced a smile as Stelios left, no doubt relieved he could now get on with welcoming genuine VIPs. We walked at a brisk pace through the now bustling departure area for the journey back south. A small group of impeccably turned out British Airways crew in starched shirts, polished shoes and crisply pressed blazers smirked as we brushed past them, their eyes lingered disdainfully and dismissively on the orange polo shirts of the easyJet cabin staff.

If the inaugural flight had been uneventful then the return trip to Luton could only be classed as a total anti-climax. But there was one big difference. In contrast to the outbound flight, the plane taking us back was only half-full. It wasn't for lack of trying on my part. A few weeks earlier I'd dropped the price of every seat in a late and unsuccessful attempt to minimise embarrassment. It was always going to be harder to fill the Glasgow to Luton route than the other way round. We'd elected to optimise the flight times for business travellers heading to Scotland rather than for their counterparts headed down south. Yet, it still didn't look good to be flying back with sixty seats unsold and I knew my boss wouldn't want to hear my excuses. At least the film crew had turned their cameras off. Stelios spent the entire flight ensconced in the cockpit and this time there was no announcement. Surveying the rows of empty seats, I reflected on the wisdom of my decision to exchange the comfort and predictability of a corporate career in the travel business for the uncertainty of an aviation start-up. How would a one-year stint working for a bankrupt airline be best covered up on my CV?

To pass the time I struck up a conversation with the elderly Scottish couple seated adjacent to me. They were on an annual pilgrimage to visit their daughter and grandchildren in Bedford. In previous years they travelled by train from Glasgow to Milton Keynes; this was the first time they'd made the journey by air, and they were impressed. My spirits lifted, these were exactly the kind of passengers easyJet would need to establish itself on the route. I made a mental note to step up our advertising at the Scottish rail stations. We landed back at Luton five minutes ahead of schedule, a 100 per cent punctuality record for our first two flights. (The thought briefly crossed my mind that had easyJet gone bust at that point, it would have become the most punctual airline in history.) This time there was no welcoming committee to greet us on the tarmac, just a cheery flight dispatcher from our handling company carrying a clipboard. The rain had finally stopped and the sun was peeking through the clouds. As passengers disembarked from the forward door, Stelios emerged from the cockpit to thank them personally for choosing to fly with his airline. His mood seemed to have lifted and his face was fixed in a broad smile as he pumped hands vigorously with the breezy confidence of a seasoned politician out canvassing votes. As we filed toward the aircraft exit, the man standing next to me in the aisle muttered under his breath, 'Don't say that guy's supposed to be the pilot. No wonder it's so cheap, he needs a haircut and where's his bloody uniform?'

'That's no pilot, darling,' exclaimed his partner knowingly, 'That's the owner, Mr Stavros whatsisname … he's Mr easyJet!'

Stelios had every right to be smiling. In getting this far he'd already beaten the odds and temporarily silenced the cynics and the sceptics. The many months of planning and hard work had paid off. His dream was alive.

Chapter Six

Trouble with travel agents

On the 18th October 1995, six weeks prior to the inaugural flight, easyJet had been officially launched with a bang at *Planet Hollywood* in London's West End. The choice of a themed fast-food eatery marked a clear departure from convention. Our judgement was that few journalists would make the trip to Luton even for the novelty value of a plucky upstart airline, so we'd make it as easy as possible for them by staging an event in Central London, throwing in free food and drink to improve turnout.

Much of what we were to announce was already in the public domain: the airline would be based at Luton, fly initially to destinations in Scotland, offer low fares, and operate Boeing 737 jet aircraft. The big secret, closely guarded from the media and the reason why so many journalists were bothering to turn up, was the headline price. Just how low could easyJet go?

It's debatable whether it was the free food and drink on offer or the quality of the story that secured a healthy turn-out of business and travel journalists. The event was timed for mid-morning, but even so we made sure that the alcohol was flowing as soon as our guests arrived, and that their glasses were regularly topped up. Stelios's sister, Clelia, made an impromptu appearance, randomly handing out orange watches from what appeared to be a Harrod's carrier bag. There was a notable buzz as the assembled crowd of hacks were ushered into the basement screening room at Planet Hollywood. When everyone was seated, Stelios took to the stage with microphone in-hand: the time had come to announce our price. Just a few days earlier in an attempt to steal easyJet's thunder, British Airways had lowered their return price to the two Scottish cities from £240 to £79. Needless to say there were a long list of accompanying conditions, and availability was strictly limited, but the bar had been well and truly lowered.

You could have heard a pin drop as Stelios cleared his throat and proudly announced that easyJet's first routes from Luton to Glasgow and Edinburgh would be priced from (cue drum-roll) £29 one way, or – as Stelios put it – 'flying for the price of a pair of jeans'. For a brief moment there was silence, then gasps and laughter from the audience. From the stage he looked out onto a sea of disbelieving faces. It was clear that pretty much everyone present was mentally writing easyJet off.

Two hours later, interviews completed, sound bites secured and the journalists having pretty much drunk the place dry, it was mission accomplished. We piled into a taxi for the journey back to Luton. The adrenaline rush of easyJet's launch was beginning to wear off and anxiety crept in. The audience's incredulous reaction when Stelios revealed our fares had dented my confidence.

The nightmare scenario would be to arrive at a silent call centre, meaning that my job would most definitely be on the line. I needn't have worried; it seemed the advertising had done its job even before the PR kicked in. By the time we burst impatiently through the doors of easyLand, the telephones were ringing off the hooks. Beaming from ear to ear, the proud owner of a newly launched airline pulled up a seat in the call centre, put on a headset and started taking bookings from his customers. In all my years working for Stelios, I don't think I ever saw him happier than at that moment.

Thumbing through the following day's press reports of the launch, I was astounded by the extent of the coverage we had achieved. Almost every national newspaper had covered our launch; little matter that collectively they had no faith in our long-term survival. What counted was that all of them had mentioned the price. Of course, by today's standards a £29 fare is nothing special, but back in 1995 it was sensational news – particularly when compared to British Airways' cheapest one-way fare, priced (until shortly before easyJet's launch) at £120. These were halcyon days in another respect: back then, there were no air passenger duties, no credit-card fees, baggage charges or priority boarding to guarantee a seat with the rest of your family. The price quoted by the telephone salesperson for your flight was the price you paid, end of story.

Despite the fact that the birth of easyJet made for good copy, we might never have made the impact we did if it wasn't for the fact that the story broke on an exceptionally quiet news day. 'Air wars over London' read the headline in the *London Evening Standard.* We'd made the front pages. What was the public reaction? Well, to put it simply, people saw the price and picked up the phone. I smiled inwardly as I recounted the words of the nameless BA spokesman: 'Europe isn't ready for the peanut airline'.

From an early stage, the benefits of selling direct became clear. We had positioned easyJet as the airline that cut out the middleman, a concept that consumers were increasingly equating with lower prices. While travel agents may not have been reviled by the great British public, they weren't exactly loved either. They were a natural target for our tongue-in-cheek advertising campaigns. 'Cut out the middleman, fly to Scotland for just £29' proclaimed our adverts in bold type above a cartoon image of a man behind a desk wearing a cheap suit and sporting a cheesy grin. 'Brown trouser time for travel agents' went one of our radio tag-lines. A stronger ad featured Stelios putting a stake through the heart of a Dracula-style cartoon agent with the strap-line: 'At easyJet, we know how to deal with bloodsuckers'. At the last minute, I bottled out from running this one. The fire we'd lit was burning brightly enough without chucking petrol on the top. The travel agency community was livid; under pressure and already faced with reductions in commission payments from the larger airlines, the insults from this insolent upstart must have been difficult to bear. Before the launch, a spokesman from the then powerful Scottish Passenger Agents Association was quoted as saying that we'd never sell a seat in Scotland without them. Several million passengers later, they were left looking pretty stupid.

Our stance on commission meant easyJet's relationship with the industry's middlemen was always going to be problematic, but no one could accuse us of failing to be up-front about where we stood. Stelios set the tone at an industry conference in Istanbul where he was asked to present to a group of senior travel agency executives. In front of a packed hall and with bodyguard watching from the side lines, he announced to a disbelieving audience, 'the relationship between us is simple: I hate you and you hate me.'

The following year, a double booking meant easyJet's founder was unable to make a scheduled repeat appearance at the Association of British Travel Agents convention in Tenerife. At short notice I was asked to step in. My late substitution in Stelios's place did not go down well; understandably delegates wanted to hear from the organ grinder not the monkey. It was the largest gathering in the trade body's history with no fewer than 2,300 travel agents in attendance. I was scared shitless – there were no heavies to back me up in the event of trouble. On arriving in the conference auditorium my first act was to check out potential escape routes. The session was entitled: 'Why easyJet will never pay commission to agents'. Discretion being the better part of valour, I skipped a slide depicting an orange meteorite headed towards a herd of dinosaurs tagged with the names of travel agency chains. The audience was silent, sullen and surly throughout. I rattled through my presentation and sat down, braced for a verbal backlash. The agents vented alright but their ire was directed not at me, but instead at the British Airways commercial director, Dan Brewin, who chose this opportunity to announce that the airline would be cutting the commission they paid to travel agents.

'At least easyJet are being honest,' a conference delegate, clearly in denial, confided to me over a beer in the hotel bar. 'BA don't seem to realise they can't survive without us.' Under the circumstances, I felt I'd got off lightly and was relieved to arrive back at Luton in one piece.

Throughout 1997, easyJet's provocation of travel agents continued and the more their representatives protested, the more we persisted in goading them. Large Ghostbusters-style posters appeared around the airport, declaring it to be a 'travel agent free zone'. Luton's marketing director, John Kingsford, complained to me that 'anti travel agent' stickers had been found stuck to the walls of the airport toilets and were proving difficult for cleaners to remove. I denied responsibility and made a mental note to order more.

Some months later, in a further escalation of hostilities, we ran a competition among our passengers to design an easyJet sick bag. The prize – a couple of free flights – was hardly a jackpot win, but we were deluged with entries. The winner submitted a suitably derogatory picture with the caption 'Sick of paying for travel agents?' We arranged for a few thousand to be printed and placed in the aircrafts' seat pockets. The operations team complained of having to constantly replace bags taken away by souvenir hunters. The campaign had been great fun, but we were making a serious point in a light-hearted way. There was simply not enough fat in the price of easyJet's flights for a middleman to take a cut.

With the airline having committed itself to the direct sales route, the choice of telephone number became a topic of heated discussion among the management team. Memorable numbers were expensive but considered vital for a direct sales business in pre-internet times. We initially settled on 01582 445566. Stelios liked the fact the number was rising "like an aircraft" The number was duly purchased from its previous owners, a local taxi company, by our hard-nosed, ex-Stelmar negotiator,

Arjun Batra, and painted in lurid orange on the aircraft fuselage. It certainly made an impact. The idea of plastering the telephone number on our planes had been my sole contribution to the development of the airline's visual identity. This design legacy first came under threat when easyJet commenced services between Luton and Amsterdam. In those days international calls attracted a hefty premium that Dutch customers were unlikely to want to pay. Securing a local Amsterdam number that could be redirected to the UK was the easy part. But what about the aircraft? The short-term solution was simple: paint the Dutch number on one side of the hull and the English number on the other. This worked as long as we were flying to a single foreign destination. However, as we continued our international expansion, the penny dropped that the concept wasn't scalable. Thankfully, the universality of the internet eventually came to the rescue and the telephone numbers were replaced with easyJet.com.

The razzmatazz of easyJet's launch barely caused a ripple in the boardrooms of Europe's aviation giants. We'd managed to get off the ground (which is more than can be said for many start-up airlines), but the idea that we posed any kind of threat to the big boys seemed laughable. Our fledgling company had just two leased Boeing 737s, which was nothing in comparison with the 250 strong BA fleet and its 300 plus routes. We now stood at a crossroads: should we take on the might of British

Airways in a no-holds barred fight, or instead adopt a less confrontational strategy, staying under their radar? For easyJet and its ambitious leader, there was only ever going to be one way forward, but the option of growing quietly and avoiding direct confrontation was a path chosen by other airline owners with more modest aspirations.

Small niche carriers had been a feature of the airline landscape for decades. Typically, these baby airlines ran operations from secondary airports, used small inefficient aircraft, charged relatively high fares and – importantly – posed no significant threat to the big guys. They brought a trickle of international transfer passengers and their existence was tolerated by big airlines in the same way that tiny fish coexist with large underwater predators by cleansing them of parasites. One such company was Suckling Airways, a small Luton-based outfit. The airline had been flying since 1986 and was run by a husband and wife team, Roy and Merlyn Suckling. Roy had been a flying instructor at Ipswich airport, while Merlyn was a qualified lawyer and by all accounts the brains of the operation. When easyJet first set up shop in Luton, Suckling Airways was operating regular scheduled flights to Amsterdam and Paris. They had a small and (what they believed to be) loyal customer base, drawn predominantly from the local catchment area. Passengers were willing to pay a premium for the convenience of Luton rather than travel round the M25 to Heathrow. There were just about enough of them to fill a propeller-driven Dornier 328 aircraft that shuttled back and forth to the continent two or three times daily. The aeroplane was noisy and cramped, seating around twenty-four passengers at full capacity.

At Stelios's insistence, I took a Suckling flight from Paris to Luton, an experience I can only describe as like riding bareback on a giant bumble bee. When easyJet commenced flights to Amsterdam in April 1996, Suckling's so-called loyal passengers deserted in droves. I must confess to feeling a twinge of guilt – even sadness – when I learned that Suckling was to stop flying from Luton and would relocate its aircraft to Cambridge airport. Oh, and if you're ever contemplating a flight on one of the smaller Dornier aircraft, bear in mind that some of them don't have toilets. Otherwise, you could end up sitting cross-legged for the entire duration of the flight – just like this author did!

It was December 1995, defying the sceptics and the prophets of doom we'd made it to our first Christmas. Anna bought a tree for the call centre and stuck an orange star on the top. It goes without saying that easyJet was losing money, but our two aircraft were shuttling up and down to Scotland carrying respectable passenger loads. A third route linking Luton with Aberdeen was already on sale and preparation for the launch of services to Amsterdam, easyJet's first destination outside the UK was at an advanced stage. Admittedly, our success owed more than a little to Lady Luck, but we were hardly complaining. With what lay ahead, easyJet would need all the luck it could get.

Chapter Seven

Hello, Boys!

The new orange airline was born on a wave of newspaper headlines and PR stunts. Yet while the deliberate courting of controversy can generate significant awareness, and is undoubtedly cost-effective, on its own it's not enough to build a brand. It took a multi-million-pound investment in above-the-line advertising to sustain easyJet and support our PR campaign at a critical stage in the airline's development. Arch rival, British Airways, had a huge advertising budget and was able to target specific routes tactically through their 'world offers' programme. From the moment we launched, it would only be a matter of time before easyJet's nemesis turned its considerable firepower on us.

For any marketing director, but particularly the marketing director of a start-up airline, determining where to spend your finite advertising budget is a vexing question. In the early days of easyJet, press advertising was our medium of choice. This was the mid-90s, and the internet was still in its infancy. The low-cost, targeted search advertising and website optimisation favoured by modern start-ups simply wasn't an option open to us. The decision to focus on press rather than broadcast advertising was not just about cost, but also had a lot to do with the constraints associated with having to secure pre-broadcast approval from the radio and TV authorities. This tended to blunt the spontaneity and topicality we had always sought to engender in our advertising. For easyJet, speed was of the essence. The stories that appeared in the previous day's newspaper columns were potential hooks for the next day's advertising. We constantly pushed the boundaries and found we could get away with a lot. The newspapers rarely rejected our ads, however provocative they might be. What's more, the Advertising Standards Authority, the body that regulated press advertising, was slow to act and had blunt teeth. In contrast, the broadcast authorities could simply refuse to approve any radio or television commercial if it failed to meet their strict criteria. And without their approval, the ad wouldn't run! Stelios was capable of controlling his temper, but watching him argue over the telephone with a faceless bureaucrat, regarding the semantics of a particular script was like witnessing the irresistible force meeting the immoveable object. On the occasions that the immoveable object triumphed, I learned to keep out of the boss's way for a few hours afterwards.

The airline's strong visual identity and simple price offer made outdoor advertising via posters and billboards a particularly effective means of getting the message across. I found a local sign writing company called *Galasso Signs*. They'd got hold of a batch of particularly lurid orange paint: not quite our official colour, but near enough. The particular shade became known as 'Sellafield orange' (after the Cumbrian town, which is home to a well-known nuclear plant), because it appeared to glow in the dark. We leased a number of large billboards in prominent sites around Luton, including one in the car park directly opposite the railway station. The hand painted designs depicted a cartoon aeroplane accompanied by the wording 'Scotland from £29'. The cheap orange paint was truly abhorrent. At the sight of the lurid billboards elderly ladies crossed themselves, young children burst spontaneously into tears and passing dogs vomited. Within a matter of days, the complaints began first to trickle and then to flood in. Some claimed that we were distracting drivers and causing accidents. One angry resident even suggested that we were impacting local property prices. Something was clearly working. New poster sites were secured, extra supplies of 'Sellafield orange' ordered in and the sign-writer was put on overtime.

In our drawn-out negotiations with Luton over landing fees, we'd persuaded the authorities to give us a significant number of prime display advertising sites around the airport free of charge. With the airport's passenger numbers stagnating there was little serious competition for the space. At the last minute, we insisted they throw in advertising on the luggage trolleys too. The car park and train station shuttle buses got the same treatment. All were adorned with the same crude (but effective) orange messaging. *Scotland for £29 with easyJet.*

Free brand advertising on trolleys and buses was nice to have, but our eyes were set on a bigger prize. Back then, and still today, any member of the public arriving or departing from Luton Airport was required to pass through a road tunnel that ran underneath the taxi-way. A huge sign, mounted immediately above the concrete underpass dominated the entrance. It was the single most impactful advertising site available and following months of persistent negotiation we finally secured it. The space was a wide horizontal strip, approximately fifteen metres in length but less than two metres high; more suited to a punchy strapline than any form of image. My preferred wording to greet millions of arriving visitors to the airport was 'Welcome to easyLand' but I was told this wouldn't be acceptable to other airlines operating from Luton. An alternative suggestion was 'You are now entering a British Airways Free Zone', but this too was deemed to be a non-starter. We settled instead for 'easy come … easy go … easyJet'.

Achieving brand domination of the airport was important but we had no intention of stopping at its perimeter. An approach was made to managers at *Thameslink*, then the franchise operator for the main rail route running south to London. We offered to repaint the scruffy waiting room at Luton train station in return for having one of our posters displayed in the station concourse. The offer was accepted, but (with a little encouragement) the contractor got a little carried away and painted one of the walls orange instead of white. Every potential branding opportunity was seized with both hands. There was an unwritten policy: if it moved, we painted it orange; if it didn't move we added an extra coat.

To Luton's inhabitants, it seemed the whole world was turning orange. I received a phone call from an indignant and irate member of the public. Refusing to identify himself he complained that 'an orange shit volcano' had erupted over his town. We had a bit of a chuckle over that one, the caller had a bad attitude, a posh accent and withheld his number, sufficient evidence for me to conclude he worked for British Airways. It was all grist to the mill. We wanted everyone passing through the area to know that easyJet had arrived and that this was our patch.

We elected not to use a full-service advertising agency, on the dual grounds of wanting to save money, and being mistrustful of middle-aged men sporting ponytails. However, we did need to work with a media-buying company. *Matters Media* was a small but fast-growing independent agency based close to the BBC offices in Marylebone, Central London. It was owned and run by Mike Hellens, an easy-going and personable character, whose wife, Abigail, worked for MTV and had known Stelios when he first arrived in London as a student. Mike may have been laid-back, but he was a shrewd businessman with a finely honed trading instinct and connections where it counted in the advertising world. His agency's success was due mainly to his having landed *Carphone Warehouse* as a client when the mobile retailer was in start-up mode a few years earlier. We'd found ourselves a great business partner. Throughout easyJet's early years, Mike and his team were at the sharp end, coping admirably with a stream of short notice requests for keenly priced advertising space to support the airline's highly tactical campaigns. Over time we became known in the market as serious buyers of distressed space; word got around amongst the advertisers that if the price was low enough then easyJet would be interested.

'Half the money I spend on advertising is wasted; the trouble is I don't know which half' is a famous quote attributed to John Wanamaker, a US department-store magnate in the 1920s. The fact that virtually all easyJet's early advertising was direct response gave us a big advantage in determining what was working. Initially, we used a single telephone number in all our ads and, as part of the booking process, call-centre staff were required to ask customers where they'd heard about easyJet, selecting the appropriate response from a drop-down list. The flaws in this approach were highlighted when an analysis of the figures revealed that the newspaper generating more calls than all the others put together was the *Aberdeen Press and Journal.* The Scottish title just happened to appear first in the alphabetically sorted drop-down list from which staff selected the responses. Lesson learned, we implemented a revised approach deploying a unique telephone number in each of our press advertising campaigns. Calls could be attributed to the paper where the ad featured. This proved a crude but surprisingly effective means of measuring advertising efficiency. We were able to focus our marketing spend on media where we believed we would get the most bang for our buck. Such a policy sounds laughably rudimentary in an age when marketers take for granted the high levels of accountability associated with internet advertising. But at the time our approach broke new ground and gave us an edge over competitors selling through travel agents. To put it another way: in the land of the blind the one-eyed orange man is king.

I made a point of putting in occasional shifts on the phones myself. I also spoke regularly with our call-centre staff to better understand how customers were learning about easyJet. There were always surprises. One of our recent recruits recounted that, when asked how he'd got hold of our telephone number, a locally based customer had responded as follows. 'I'd heard about easyJet on the radio but never thought much about it till the day came when I needed to book a flight. I was mowing my lawn when one of your planes flew over my garden … seeing the number written on the side, I rushed into the house, grabbed a pen and wrote it down!'

Prior to my joining easyJet Stelios had invited a prestigious London agency to come up with design concepts for his airline. He found their ideas uninspiring and was profoundly unimpressed by the accompanying price tag. Acting on Stelios's instructions I drew up a shortlist of less expensive agencies. They duly pitched their ideas but none seemed able to capture the essence of the brand he wanted to create. It was clear to me that what Stelios really wanted was to sit over the shoulder of an Apple Mac operator who translate the ideas in his head to a screen. A different approach was needed. I trawled through the local edition of the Yellow Pages phone directory and found a small, local design and print company called *White Knight Design*. We wanted low-cost and that's exactly what we got. This was no West-End advertising agency boudoir stuffed with pampered creative types. Nor were they paying over the odds for cool-looking dudes. Our account manager bore a striking resemblance to Postman Pat. The company was keen, capable and hungry for our business. Located on what was then a run-down industrial estate a short drive from the airport, their office was accessed through a steel door, like a crack den. They told me it had been installed following a daylight raid by balaclava-wearing robbers wielding baseball bats.

And so, in late July1995, in this refreshingly ‘luvvie-free zone’, the easyJet visual identity was born. I sat next to Stelios, huddled round an Apple Mac with lead designer Barry Debenham. Stelios was firmly in control of the design process. A template of a Boeing 737-200 aircraft, viewed from the side, was displayed on the screen. He kicked different concepts around before finally coming up with the airline’s distinctive Cooper-Black font and orange tail livery. When Barry superimposed the name *EasyJet* on the aircraft tail fin, Stelios asked him to write it with a small ‘e’ and a large ‘J’. I pulled a face at the suggestion, but viewed on the screen, I had to admit, it looked right. To emphasise the airline’s direct sell credentials I came up with the idea of putting our telephone number on the side of the plane. It was as simple as that. By my reckoning a design agency would have taken a month and charged at least £50,000 for the privilege. Instead Stelios had conjured up a visual identity in a matter of hours, we had successfully applied it to easyJet’s first aircraft and the cost was next to nothing.

The passing of this particular milestone meant we could get on with crafting advertising to pull in the punters. The messages were simple and direct: always featuring the price, one or more destinations and a call to action. The design style was simplistic, unsubtle, bordering on childish; cartoon depictions of the aircraft featured in the earliest ads. They were crudely drawn and more than a little cringe-worthy: plane with clogs for Holland; plane with a beret for France; plane with sombrero (yes, I know its Mexican) for Spain. Thank God for Ryanair whose ads were even cheaper, nastier and naffer than ours. It was the design equivalent of a race to the bottom with the Irish airline eventually running out worthy winners.

Time passed, and, perhaps inevitably, things moved on. Cartoon representations of the easyJet aircraft gave way first to line drawings and eventually to photographs. It had become apparent that many of our potential customers were unaware of one of our biggest strengths: the relatively young age of our aeroplanes. Indeed, at a rare research focus group session a number of the participants, none of whom had previously flown with us, revealed that they thought easyJet operated old propeller-driven aircraft. It was a valuable insight and Stelios was quick to pick up on the marketing potential of having a comparatively young fleet. Not long after we'd got rid of our older leased aircraft and replaced them with shiny brand-new Boeings, this was developed into a key advertising theme. I was struck by the reaction of first-time easyJet fliers, pleasantly surprised by the shiny new aeroplanes on which they were travelling. Exceeding limited customer expectations is what being a successful low-cost airline is about.

With a rise in the frequency of services on our Anglo-Scottish routes Stelios was effectively doubling down on his original bet. Filling our planes now required us to grow the market, it was not enough to grab share from existing operators. Implicitly, this meant attracting passengers who would normally use the railways. We singled out infrastructure operator Railtrack and the train operators for some serious treatment. They proved a good target. The newly privatised railway companies were unloved, vilified in the media and regarded with considerable suspicion by the general public.

Back in 1996, the rail franchise for the East Coast main line between London and Scotland was operated by an outfit who called themselves GNER. It sounded less like the name of a train company, more like the noise you make when a cricket ball hits you between the legs. The fact they had recently appointed Lorraine Flower, a former British Airways executive, as their marketing director, provided an added incentive for easyJet to play hardball. I drew up plans for an aggressive poster campaign that would highlight the price differences between plane and train. I anticipated there might be a request to tone down the advertising copy, but there were dark forces at work. When we tried to secure prime sites at London's Kings Cross and Edinburgh's Waverley stations, there was a sudden and mysterious lack of availability. It looked like someone had been tipped off.

Undeterred, we decided on a different angle of attack. Tapping into a high-profile news story, we took out full-page ads in the *London Evening Standard* and the Scottish press depicting a cartoon snail looking aghast at a large leaf on the line under the heading 'notsoeasy train'. It was to become known as the 'Snailtrack' ad. Humour must have been a commodity in short supply in the rail industry, for we received a letter from GNER, containing a polite request (which, needless to say, we ignored) to desist. According to the letter, our advertisements 'were causing considerable offence'. This was but one of a number of instances where requests for the withdrawal of advertisements led to the extension of the life of a campaign. The ad was printed out, framed and fixed to the wall behind Stelios's desk at easyLand, with the picture of the cartoon travel agent alongside. A pattern was starting to emerge.

Working in a grotty tin shack helped keep the marketing team grounded, but we got the occasional glimpse of the glitzy circles in which our contemporaries at British Airways were moving. In early 1996 I paid a visit with Stelios to the plush West End offices of advertising firm Howell Henry Chaldecott Lury (HHCL). We were there to discuss a potential tie-up with their client, the soft drink brand *Tango*. The meeting was a timely reminder of the indulgences of West End agencies and the money easyJet was saving through its low-cost approach to marketing. HHCL were reportedly the only advertising agency to employ both a futurologist and a shaman. Their air-conditioned office was stuffed with cool-looking people lounging around and talking to one another. None of them seemed to be doing any actual work. I counted three middle-aged men in ponytails, two glamorous blonde PR types wearing sunglasses indoors (a no-no unless you're Italian) and a bearded hipster who'd fallen through a time warp from twenty years in the future.

Before the meeting even started we were made to sit through a self-congratulatory presentation of the agency's credentials. It was painful to endure, especially the video clip of HHCL executives delivering acceptance speeches, quaffing champagne and high-fiving one another at a high-profile award ceremony. The agency were on the crest of a wave following their famous, controversial and – as they continually reminded us – multi award-winning 'You've been Tango'd' advertising campaign. The idea we brought to the table was that an easyJet plane could be 'Tango'd' with a giant orange splash. Their executives liked the idea but scoffed at the notion their client might actually pay easyJet for any collaborative brand project. A couple of patronising remarks later, Stelios had heard enough. I found myself back on the street outside the HHCL office breathing in deep lungful's of fresh, bullshit-free air. It had been a learning experience. With such extravagance on open display it was no surprise to learn a couple of years later that HHCL had been hired to work on British Airway's own low-cost airline project.

With the passage of time, we can now look back and appreciate the full extent of the changes that have taken place in the world of airline marketing. Since easyJet first burst onto the scene, the battleground has shifted away from traditional media towards the world of digital, social and mobile marketing. It's no understatement to say that the arrival of the internet changed airline advertising for ever. Printed media has become a largely irrelevant slideshow. Along with most of its competitors, easyJet today spends the lion's share of its now multi-million-pound annual marketing budget online. Search-based advertising, social media and a proliferation of intermediary sites allow the smallest of start-ups with the most modest of budgets to make their offering available to prospective customers around the globe. Through judicious selection of search terms, money can be targeted at a specific route or a particular competitor. Every click a customer makes and every penny the advertiser spends can be measured and reported on a real-time basis. The idea of making airline advertising accountable, pioneered all those years ago by easyJet, has truly come of age.

Chapter Eight

Football crazy

The movie *Brewster's Millions* was a minor hit in the late 80s. The main character, played by actor Richard Pryor, is a down-and-out baseball player who has to burn his way through $30 million in thirty days in order to inherit his true fortune of $300 million. Not only was it a great movie, it was also cult viewing among the easyJet management team. Starting an airline is undoubtedly a great way to dissipate a Brewster-sized fortune, but one of the few alternative ways of burning cash at a comparable rate is to become involved with the world of football.

Polys Haji-Ioannou is the older brother of Stelios. Rather than blazing a trail in a new industry, he followed in the footsteps of his father and became a shipping magnate. Nick Manoudakis had pre-warned me: Polys is crazy about football and in particular is a keen supporter of north London side Tottenham Hotspur.

It was difficult to turn down the chairman's brother particularly since he was also a substantial shareholder in easyJet. One cold evening in December 1997, Polys invited me to watch Tottenham play Chelsea from the comfort of the White Hart Lane director's box. I was excited by the prospect of going to the match, but not looking forward to batting away persistent sponsorship enquiries from the club's commercial director Mike Rollo. We were still in the early stages of building the easyJet brand and our budget was deployed almost exclusively on direct response advertising. I was trying to squeeze every last penny of value from the budget. Sports sponsorship at any level, let alone the English Premier League, was difficult to justify. To make things worse, Tottenham were going through a bad patch and languishing in the bottom half of the table. The finance director's parting words as I headed out the door were ringing in my ears. "Don't drink anything, don't agree to anything and above all make sure you don't sign anything.'

Despite the home team's recent bad run of form, the Spurs fans had high expectations. My taxi-driver told me he had £10 riding on a 2-1 Tottenham victory. His confidence was misplaced. They were totally outplayed by a rampant Chelsea who triumphed by six goals to one. The players left the pitch to a chorus of whistles and catcalls. With the side having received such a hammering no one seemed inclined to talk about sponsorship. It was a very bad night for Tottenham, but a good one for the marketing budget. The highlight of the evening was a post-match conversation with midfielder David Ginola, the only member of the home team to have played with any passion or conviction. The French international told me he used easyJet every couple of weeks to travel from his north London home to visit his family in the south of France. I took encouragement from the fact we were starting to attract customers whose pockets were deep enough to pay the high fares of British Airways or Air France, but instead chose to fly with easyJet.

Rather than spending the airlines advertising money on the 'beautiful game', I saw it as an area of significant sales opportunity. A steep rise in the number of European club matches and the success of British teams on the continental stage was generating significant demand for cheap flights, particularly in the winter months when holiday traffic fell away. Not only that but kick-off for these games was typically around 8pm. As far as easyJet was concerned, this was perfect timing. Unlike business travellers whose companies favoured an early start, football fans preferred to set off in the late morning or early afternoon. These were the flights that airlines often struggled to fill.

The geography of football, by which I mean the various European cup competitions, also worked in our favour. Three of the UK's biggest football cities – Liverpool, Manchester and (North) London – were within easy travelling distance of an easyJet airport and we were determined to grab a share of this burgeoning market. In the first couple of years, before the airline's revenue-management became fully automated, I recall vividly the real-time choreography surrounding the Champions League draw. A small group were seated in a tight circle around a desktop computer. On the table were a pair of speakers, relaying Radio 5 Live's coverage at full volume. The computer was logged directly into the pricing tables that lay at the heart of the easyJet booking system. No-one spoke, the only sound that mattered was coming from the speakers in front of us. John's finger would be poised, ready to adjust fares depending on the fixtures revealed while, hundreds of miles away, the team names were drawn from the hat.

We learned from experience that football fans moved quickly to secure their travel arrangements, and we weren't the only ones with our fingers poised over keyboards. It was a bit like a Wild West shoot-out. Unless we reacted and adjusted our prices immediately, flights could sell out in a matter of minutes – sometimes, in seconds. Every year the draw for the European tournaments brought easyJet a minor financial windfall. The 1998/99 season was particularly lucrative with Manchester United playing Barcelona both home and away in the group stages and then beating Bayern Munich in a memorable final staged at the Catalan stadium. In the space of a few hours following the announcement of fixtures for each round there were dramatic inflows of revenue as both sets of supporters flocked to secure their flights. It was tempting to rack prices up as high as they would go, but at this early stage in the development of the easyJet brand we were careful not to overdo it.

When it came to travel planning, football supporters were a canny bunch. Even before the advent of social media they operated an informal but extremely efficient communications network that facilitated the sharing of pricing and transport information at lightning speed. A cat and mouse battle developed between budget-conscious soccer fans and the yield management department based at easyLand. In their struggle to get the best possible prices, the fans were working out creative new ways to beat the system. As the low-cost airlines expanded at an accelerating pace, many more points on the European map became linked to a vast, inter-connecting budget network. At its simplest, being a successful low-cost airline means moving large numbers of people from point A to point B and, of course, varying fares appropriately, depending on the level of demand at any given point in time. However, the proliferation of low-cost routes meant that, in certain circumstances, flying from point A to point B via point C might actually be cheaper than flying from A to B direct.

The *Telegraph*'s website cited the case of a journey from Bournemouth to Glasgow where the quickest way to reach the

Scottish city was not by car or train, but to travel on Ryanair via Barcelona. The twist in this particular tale was that diverting to the continent was not only faster, but cheaper too. Football fans were quick to work out these alternative routings, causing problems not only for airline revenue managers, but also for their counterparts in the rail industry. The same *Telegraph* story reported how a Liverpool football fan from north London flew from London to Liverpool via Brussels to watch his team play against Aston Villa. Amazingly, the flights ended up costing him less than half the price of a return train ticket. Andy Rolle and his friend, Chris, apparently paid £100 for two return flights. This compared with the £204 Virgin Trains wanted for two return tickets to Merseyside. The two men arrived at Stansted airport in Essex at 6.45 a.m. for a 7.30 a.m. flight, landed in Brussels an hour later and took a flight to Liverpool an hour after that, arriving at 11.45 a.m. 'It was perfect,' Mr Rolle said, 'especially when we beat Villa one nil. But it's the first time I've needed my passport to see Liverpool play at Anfield.'

There was an obvious temptation for easyJet to put on extra flights in order to capitalise on the excess demand resulting from one-off sports events. In May 1997 this backfired in spectacular fashion when we elected to add an extra additional service to accommodate passengers returning to Luton from Nice, following the Monaco Grand Prix. It is a common misconception that airlines have spare aircraft sitting idle on the tarmac waiting to be used. In reality, other than short spells on the ground to load and off-load passengers, all easyJet's planes flew pretty much non-stop between 6 in the morning and 11 at night. The only way we could operate an additional rotation down to Nice and back on a Sunday evening was by cancelling a scheduled flight on another route. But which one should we choose? The obvious candidate was Aberdeen, a predominantly business destination where leisure traffic at weekends was relatively light and yields consequently low. A full planeload of passengers returning to Luton following the Grand Prix could yield £20,000 more than operating the scheduled service to Scotland. It looked to be a straightforward swap. Almost a no-brainer, what could possibly go wrong? There were no dissenting voices among the management team, so we went for it.

Several weeks prior to the date in question, the necessary changes were made in the easyJet booking system. The flights between Luton and Aberdeen were removed from sale and a handful of pre-booked passengers refunded. The extra rotation to Nice was duly loaded. All seats were offered at the highest price; this was not a charitable gesture. It appeared to be working like a dream. Within a few days we'd sold all 148 seats for the Nice to London leg at £199 each generating over £29,000 for easyJet's coffers. It was the most profitable single flight in the airline's history. Or rather it would have been the most profitable single flight had the commercial team informed the flight operations department of the schedule change. What an almighty fuck-up! One balmy Sunday afternoon on 11th May 1997, an easyJet flight left Luton bound for Aberdeen totally empty and returned a couple of hours later also with zero passengers on board. Meanwhile 148 passengers were stranded, with steam coming out of their ears, at Nice airport. Among them were a number of wealthy and well-connected individuals, including at least one chief executive of a major UK company. There was virtually no prospect of getting them home without paying through the nose on a rival scheduled service or chartering in capacity at huge expense. John Macleod later told me it had been one hell of a shit-storm to clear up, Stelios was not amused.

Chapter Nine

Dare to be different

Anyone passing through Luton Airport towards the end of 1995 need only have looked about them for evidence that easyJet was visibly and undeniably different. It wasn't just the distinctive orange lettering on its planes, the telephone number writ large on the aircraft hull and the lurid uniforms of the cabin crew that caused the young upstart to stand out from its peers. We'd intentionally set out to create a fundamentally different kind of airline, a company where questioning the established way of doing things was the norm.

Being the world's first carrier to go one hundred per cent direct saved us a small fortune in travel agents' commission and booking fees. This crucial decision also allowed easyJet to operate as a ticketless airline from day one, generating further savings on printing, postage and accounting for tickets. To make things simple, we took a firm line with customers whose arrangements changed. Once a flight was booked, cancellations and refunds were not permitted. Pampered business travellers paying BA's high fares were accustomed to an element of flexibility. They found the 'use it or lose it' policy hard to take. We became accustomed to squeals of indignation and howls of outrage from those whose requests had been turned down. A customer told me the only difference between the respective policies of Ryanair and ourselves, was that we would tell people they couldn't have a refund *politely*.

Compared with conventional airlines, easyJet's aircraft were highly utilised, flying from early in the morning until late at night. Speedy twenty to thirty minute turnarounds (the time the plane spends on the tarmac between flights) and the simplicity of our operating model allowed easyJet to 'sweat' its most expensive assets. Traditional airline boarding cards were replaced with bright orange, re-usable laminated boarding tags numbered consecutively from 1 to 130. Not only did this save on paper, it also provided an incentive for passengers to show up early for check-in, aware they would boarded in numerical order. The back of the boarding tags were awash with advertising.

Starting with a blank sheet of paper, we looked for savings everywhere we could find them. The only exception was safety, which could never be compromised. Stelios had experienced the trauma of a major accident some years previously when an oil tanker called *The Haven*, leased by his father's shipping company Troodos, had blown-up with loss of life, causing a major pollution incident off the Italian coastline. There followed a legal battle in the Italian courts that dragged on for many years, with Stelios and his father facing manslaughter charges before being fully and finally acquitted on all counts in 2002. Unsurprisingly, the commitment of easyJet's owner to running a safe operation was absolute. As if it were needed, a stark reminder of the safety imperative came in May 1996 with the crash of ValuJet flight 592 into the Florida Everglades resulting in the death of everyone on board. It was a pretty sobering moment for all of us.

Safety aside, pretty much everything else was fair game when it came to cost cutting. The complimentary on-board meals that were *de rigueur* back in those days were an early casualty. Quite what had persuaded a generation of European airlines that passengers needed something to eat on flights of such short duration, I will never know. British Airways prided itself on the hot breakfasts available on its early morning flights from London to Scotland. An urban myth had developed that soggy bacon, shrivelled mushroom and reconstituted scrambled egg was a significant factor in the business traveller's choice of airline. The cost of providing such a service in the air was a multiple of what it cost on the ground. We had no intention of perpetuating such madness. Stelios developed a fondness for the saying 'there's no such thing as a free lunch', and so it proved as he introduced *easyKiosk*, one of the earliest extensions of the easy brand. The service was run in partnership with Alpha in-flight catering, who became the first brand licensee. Before long easyJet was making a tidy profit, selling drinks and snacks that competitors were giving away for free. When British Airway's catering staff voted to go out on strike, we issued a solemn undertaking that our non-existent catering staff would never follow suit. As the revenues from on-board sales grew, competitors began to first sit up and take notice, and then to follow easyJet's example. Their free on-board meals became progressively more modest, before, in many cases, disappearing all together.

It's the visible differences that stick most in the memory. In the mid-90s the uniforms of UK short-haul cabin crew could best be described as bland, formulaic and unadventurous. Here was an obvious opportunity for easyJet to carve out a distinctive identity for itself. Once again we looked over the pond for inspiration. North American carriers, naturally Southwest Airlines among them, had already demonstrated that casual cabin crew uniforms were welcomed by passengers and staff alike. Of course we had to take the British weather into account. The baggy shorts favoured in the Texas climate would probably be less acceptable to a crew member disembarking passengers on a cold, windy, February morning in Aberdeen.

We started out with very few preconceptions other than a desire to stand out from the crowd and to keep the uniform costs as low as possible. We'd had expressions of interest from a number of suppliers who liked the idea of kitting out an airline. The bidders included a married couple who claimed to have designed Lady Diana's wedding dress. In the summer of 1995, they came to easyLand to present their ideas and their prices – and went away empty-handed. In traditional easyJet style, we thought we could do better ourselves. Not only that: buying something 'off the shelf' would mean significantly lower cost. We had to start somewhere. I made a trip with Stelios to the *Next* clothing store in the town of Harpenden, a few miles down the road from Luton. We made for an unlikely couple. As he walked slowly through the shop Stelios pointed at various items of clothing that caught his eye. 'I don't care about the size,' he said to the bemused shop assistant. We loaded my car up with a selection of jackets, shirts and trousers, before driving back to easyLand, where staff took part in an impromptu catwalk session. The verdict was a unanimous and unequivocal thumbs-down. The outfits may have been casual, but they were insufficiently distinctive and failed to capture the imagination. We'd also learned there were Civil Aviation Authority rules in place covering the use of synthetic fabrics for crew uniforms, presumably in case of fire. It was back to the drawing board and time was not on our side.

Then out of the blue, Anna Zioura, our ultra-efficient office manager, mentioned that she'd seen someone wandering through Luton town centre wearing a striking orange polo shirt bearing a Benetton logo. On the strength of her sighting, I was dispatched to the nearest Benetton shop, located half an hour up the M1 in Milton Keynes. It was true: there was a polo shirt and a matching sweatshirt, both items in garish easyJet orange, matching the 'official' colour almost perfectly. Excited by my discovery, I called the boss. Stelios was in a meeting but instructed me to return immediately to easyLand, pick him up and take him to Milton Keynes. I had my foot on the accelerator all the way. When he saw the shirts, Stelios had no hesitation: he pulled out his credit card and duly bought all the orange polos and sweatshirts in the shop. There were around eight of each, in a variety of different sizes. As soon as we arrived back at easyLand, there was a second 'fashion show'. This time feedback from the team was overwhelmingly positive. Everyone wanted to try the new shirts on. What's more, the garments were manufactured from pure cotton and therefore met with Civil Aviation Authority requirements.

There was no time to lose. The clock counting down the days to easyJet's inaugural flight continued to tick remorselessly. I immediately set about trying to place an order for a couple of hundred identical shirts from Benetton's wholesaling arm in Italy. This proved more difficult than anticipated. It transpired that Benetton did not keep much in the way of central stock, particularly of gaudy colours like orange that go out of fashion as quickly as they come in. Undeterred, I undertook a fast-paced road trip around London and the South East visiting a large number of Benetton stores, including outlets in Islington, Brent Cross and Oxford Street. It's hard to imagine quite what the shop staff made of this eccentric character that ran in, tried nothing on but swept all the orange sweatshirts and polo shirts off the racks and stuffed them into a large kit bag. By the end of my UK shopping tour, I had accumulated around one hundred and fifty shirts of various sizes, three sets of uniform per cabin crew member. There was no way of getting hold of more in time for the first flight. I took an inventory and worked out that in our recruitment drive, which was already underway, we'd need to find twelve 'Large', twenty 'Medium' and eighteen 'Small' members of cabin crew to fit the uniforms I'd purchased. Finding sufficient crew for our two aircraft fleet proved not to be a problem, though a couple of otherwise well-qualified candidates missed out because their measurements failed to align with the remaining supply of uniforms.

I was determined the marketing department would be run in a very different fashion to British Airways. What easyJet lacked in staff numbers, experience and financial resources, we would make up for with creativity, energy and enthusiasm. By mid-1997, the weekly marketing meetings had become a focal point for the airline's commercial activities. Most of the country managers were based overseas and would fly into Luton on the previous night. Each of them came to the meeting armed with the very latest information, gathered on the ground in their respective markets. The session started with an analysis of the previous week's sales data provided by revenue manager, John Stevenson. We pored over charts and graphs, debated forward booking patterns and analysed pricing curves to identify where we needed to focus our marketing attention. The fact we were selling direct to our passengers rather than via travel agents gave easyJet a depth and quality of data that BA's marketing team would have killed for. Then, based on consideration of the data and the market manager's insights, we took decisions. Our analytical tools might have been complex but the underlying principles were simple; understand what's happening, spot trends early, if something works, do more of it, should something not work then stop doing it.

They were great years. It was a highly productive and stimulating working environment. The easyJet commercial team was young, bright, and close-knit. Several of them were former students of nearby Cranfield University, which offered a postgraduate course in Air Transport Management. Our meetings were structured and business-like, but they could also be hugely enjoyable - often punctuated with humour. If he was available then Stelios would attend. In fact, it was he who introduced the dubious innovation of holding the meetings standing up 'to keep them short'. Truth be told, the meetings ran on twice as long when the airline's founder was in attendance. After two or three hours, participants would be leaning on chairs, walls or whatever came to hand. If Stelios left the meeting for any reason, we all immediately sat down. I kept a battery-powered soft toy gorilla safely locked away in the drawer of my desk. Originally bought as a present for my five-year-old nephew, he'd taken one look and burst into tears. Its menacing features, slightly crazed eyes and stocky build meant it bore more than a passing resemblance to easyJet's founder. The gorilla's first appearance was made during a discussion of the Spanish routes, which is how our furry friend came to acquire the nickname 'El Stel'. When switched on, it would shuffle around making squawking noises and waving its arms in an animated fashion. Bringing out the gorilla was a great way to lighten the mood when 'The Supreme Leader' was out of town.

It would be ludicrous to claim that throwing mass parties, bringing the airline's staff together to celebrate and let off steam was in any way an easyJet invention. Virgin, Southwest and, to be fair, a number of conventional airlines, had a reputation for partying hard. But it was hardly surprising that large-scale parties rapidly became a highlight of the easyJet social calendar. The first such event was staged on the eve of our launch in *Blues West Fourteen*, a basement blues club in West Kensington. It was a high-spirited affair and those present danced the night away into the small hours. There was a significant contingent from the call centre, all of whom made it into work the next morning. Those early days also saw memorable parties at the chairman's homes in both London and Monaco, though these were not to last as Stelios drew a firm dividing line between his personal and public lives.

As easyJet grew so the staff parties increased in size, with an abundance of creative thinking, planning and preparation involved. Such events came to be viewed as an investment in the airline's people rather than indulgent expenditure. The space-themed party staged at a Bedfordshire airfield was a night to remember. An employee dressed as a giant alien on stilts wielding a 'British Airways Blaster' ray gun greeted guests as they arrived. With hundreds of staff attending, many of them unfamiliar faces, it was brought home to me that we were no longer a small company. By now the majority of operational staff and crew were based in a separate office away from easyLand. The parties were a place where the whole orange family could get together. This wasn't just about indulgence and staff letting their hair down, it had become an integral part of our organisational culture. You might think that partying at easyJet was no different from British Airways, but we seemed to have a magic ingredient – and sometimes there could be unanticipated business benefits.

In late 1996, we'd decided to throw our biggest staff party yet at Luton. The exact cause of celebration escapes me now (in fact, we didn't always need a reason!). It had become the norm for invitations to be extended to local business partners, including suppliers and airport handling staff. On this particular occasion we were joined by half a dozen baggage handlers from Glasgow airport where airlines including easyJet had been experiencing delays related to slow processing of hold luggage. The group had been flown down to Luton free of charge on seats that would otherwise have been empty.

With the party in full swing, I approached one of our Glaswegian guests. He held a pint glass in his hand raising a toast to easyJet and was swaying unsteadily on his feet. My new best friend told me, in a broad accent and in no uncertain terms, that this was the first time any airline had invited 'the likes of them' to a party. Airport baggage handlers had a reputation for militancy, but on this occasion the decision to invite them proved to be an inspired one. I'm convinced that for months following the party, baggage from easyJet flights flew off the airport conveyor belts more rapidly than those of our competitors.

Many of easyJet's formative commercial decisions shared a common characteristic in that they were things that British Airways would never have contemplated. An obvious example is the 'Airline' TV programme. In 1998 we were approached by

London Weekend Television, a production company seeking permission to film a 'fly on the wall' documentary series. Stelios immediately called a meeting of the management team in the easyLand boardroom to debate the pros and cons. He went around the table and asked all those in attendance what they thought. A range of views were expressed; the majority were against. I could see what was coming. There was a gleam in his eye that told me there was only ever going to be one decision.

The first series of 'Airline' to feature the budget carrier aired on ITV in January 1999. It proved an instant hit, attracting audiences of up to ten million viewers. A large part of the UK viewing population tuned in for their weekly dose of *schadenfreude* (a term of Germanic origin meaning delight in another's misfortune). At one point the programme was running third in the national TV rankings behind blockbusters *Coronation Street* and *EastEnders*. The public, it seemed, was captivated and entranced by the sight of irate passengers dealing with delays, lost baggage and the thousand and one other things that can conceivably go wrong at an airport. A number of easyJet employees were thrust into the limelight, in some cases becoming reality TV stars overnight. While they revelled in their fifteen minutes of fame, the number of applications for jobs with the airline soared still further.

Giving the cameras unfettered, behind-the-scenes access to their operations in this way would have been inconceivable to the majority of companies. In easyJet's case, it was a calculated gamble, typical of Stelios's buccaneering style. The exposure gave the airline an unprecedented level of brand awareness, not just in the UK, but also in many overseas markets where the documentary has subsequently aired. Sceptics still contend that to show easyJet passengers experiencing travel-related traumas casts the airline in a negative light. In my view, the viewing public is sufficiently intelligent to understand that 'passenger shows up, checks in and arrives on time after an uneventful flight' doesn't make for great television.

Saving money and generating publicity weren't the only considerations in our ongoing efforts to do things differently. We had a big communications job on our hands. Customers needed to understand how easyJet was able to offer lower fares without compromising safety. It was important we relayed this important message as concisely and effectively as possible. Simplicity was crucial. There are many differences between the business models of a low-cost and a full-service airline that collectively account for the price differential. From a marketing standpoint, we focussed on three that the public found it easy to understand: cutting out the travel agent; using Luton rather than Heathrow; and not serving up a free meal on board the plane. These key themes were developed into appropriate creative executions and deployed in the early advertising campaigns. Coupled with a strategy of showing off easyJet's modern fleet of aircraft at every possible opportunity, this sent a clear and coherent message to customers. We were saving money by cutting out the things they didn't need rather than compromising their safety.

The mettle of any company is only truly tested in the face of adversity. The devastating attacks of September 11th 2001 proved a turning point for the low-cost sector in general and easyJet in particular. Overnight the global aviation industry was brought to its knees. British Airways reacted instinctively by cutting back on capacity, a policy that had served them well in previous crises. In November 2001 as part of the airline's retrenchment they slashed their programme of flights from Gatwick by 25%. The airport had long been capacity constrained but following BA's move, take-off and landing slots became available for the first time in a decade. While others dithered, easyJet seized their chance, bagging dozens of prime slots and announcing new routes to Edinburgh, Zurich, Palma and Malaga. Furthermore it was announced that Gatwick was to become the airline's main base and a centre of aircraft operations. It was a typically decisive and opportunistic move. By the time the civil aviation industry had regrouped and resumed something approaching normal operations, the deal was done and easyJet's significant presence at Gatwick had been well and truly cemented.

Incorporating fresh thinking when you're starting a new business clearly makes sense, but in reality nearly every new idea can be copied and so it has proved. Online sales, automated check-in and the generation of ancillary revenue are today common denominators across the industry. We were the first airline to put our web address on the side of the aircraft but others were quick to follow suit. Just as we learned and borrowed from our American predecessors, so others that followed later did the same to easyJet. In this way the game of corporate Darwinism plays out. Standing still simply isn't an option in an industry as fast moving as civil aviation. History proves you need to constantly question everything you're doing, and look outside both your own organisation and the industry in which you operate for inspiration.

If the easyJet team had a secret ingredient, it was that we had no fear of failure. Setting up a new airline is akin to opening a garden centre in the Sahara Desert. The expectations of success are limited, you are willing to take considerable business risks and your survival instincts become sharply tuned. On the rare occasions that an airline beats the odds and becomes successful, its history is written through the prism of that success. Inconvenient truths that fail to fit the narrative have a tendency to be glossed over. There were countless occasions, some of them documented in this book that we fell flat on our faces. We learned to pick ourselves up, dust off our clothes and carry on. The trick was to fail early, learn the lessons, and move on.

Pretty much every company history I've read underplays the extent of the impact a positive organisational culture can have on long-term business outcomes. In contrast they invariably overestimate the significance of strategic planning and overstate the value added by senior executives. Management consultant and business guru, Peter Drucker, was an observer and ardent admirer of Southwest airlines. He concluded that focusing energy and investment on developing a powerful and enabling culture constitutes a surer route to organisational success than having a well-honed and competently executed business plan. I've long been a fan of Drucker's work and have come to believe he had Southwest very much in mind when he famously uttered the words that 'culture eats strategy for breakfast'.

Chapter Ten

Luton Airport

I've been described as 'laid-back' often enough for me to accept the label neither as a strength nor a weakness but simply as a statement of fact. There is a short list of things that truly wind me up. On that list – alongside fly tippers, Ryanair, and people who like their own status on Facebook – you will find the group of companies who manage Britain's biggest and busiest airports. In my view they bear ultimate responsibility for the purgatory endured on a daily basis by millions of departing passengers. Over a period of years airports have been fundamentally reconfigured by masochistic accountants, forcing customers to walk through a bewildering array of retail concessions on their way to the aircraft. What the hell is wrong with these people? I'm reminded of journalist Matt Taibbi's infamous description of investment bank *Goldman Sachs* as being 'a vampire squid wrapped around the face of humanity, relentlessly jamming its blood funnel into anything that smells like money'. Four pounds for a thirty second drop-off in the immediate vicinity of the terminal and a tenner for a couple of Toblerones, really? Give me a break!

It wasn't always like that. There was a time when it cost just £4.50 to park right next to the airport for a whole day. Refreshments were a straight choice between a KFC concession, an airside bar with Guinness on tap and an Irish-themed coffee shop. A complimentary bus service operated from the airport to the train station, manned by a friendly team of local drivers who'd step in to help at the sight of passengers struggling with their luggage.

In fact, when easyJet struck their deal to come to Luton in 1995, the airport was both owned and operated by Luton Borough Council. It was also deeply in debt and heavily loss making. Within three years, thanks largely to easyJet, traffic had more than doubled from 1.8 million to over 4 million travellers a year. Further substantial growth in passenger numbers was anticipated, and something had to be done to accommodate them.

Expansion of the airport undoubtedly brought jobs and opportunity to a town with pockets of significant deprivation. But there was a price to be paid in terms of traffic congestion, increased rents and for those living on the proposed new flightpaths, aircraft noise. Residents groups particularly those drawing from the more affluent towns and villages bordering Luton were vocal in their opposition. One of the airport's directors told me he had attended a public meeting where the airports plans were being presented. The venue for the consultation was picketed by a sizeable contingent of local property owners waving placards and chanting in opposition. He was surprised to count at least three easyJet employees among them. When challenged it was explained they were not opposed to airport expansion per se, only to the flight path coming anywhere near their houses.

For as long as the day-to-day management of the airport remained in the hands of Luton Borough Council, well organised opponents stood a chance of slowing or even stymying its growth. But the rules of the game were about to change. In 1997 to facilitate the necessary infrastructure investment, the council issued a 30-year concession contract to a public-private partnership consortium, jointly owned by *Airports International Group* and *Barclays Private Equity*. Anyone standing in the way of Luton's growth was now coming up against powerful corporate interests backed by an army of lobbyists and legal advisers.

Construction of a brand-new terminal was to be the centrepiece of Luton's development. This would be no ordinary building, but an aluminium and glass cathedral with an estimated price tag of £40 million. It was based on an original design by no less a person than the multi-award-winning architect, Sir Norman Foster. To put it mildly, easyJet was alarmed by the prospect of such extravagance. While the airline acknowledged the need to upgrade the airport infrastructure, it sought a more functional facility, designed to cater for the smooth and efficient processing of millions of low-cost passengers. 'What you guys want is an easyShed,' said one of Luton airport's managers disparagingly, in an unguarded moment, perhaps anticipating an indignant denial in response. That's exactly what we want, I thought to myself.

The lion's share of the bill for the proposed architectural indulgence would be picked up by, you guessed it, easyJet. In revitalising Luton, we had become victims of our own success. The battle to stop the development of what Stelios took to calling 'The Taj Mahal' was fought largely behind the scenes for the next year and a half. But things flared up dramatically in early 1999 with the 'outing' of Barclays Bank as a leading member of the consortium providing the development financing.

In May 2000 *The Times* reported the airport intended to raise landing fees from £1.68 per passenger to between £6 and £7, an increase that would make a significant dent in easyJet's profitability. While toys were being thrown out of the orange pram, construction work continued apace. In November 1999, a shiny new passenger terminal was opened by Prince Philip and Her Majesty The Queen. The official ceremony was boycotted by easyJet in protest at what it called 'an airport management hell-bent on wrecking Luton airport and returning it to the days of Lorraine Chase'.

For easyJet, the involvement of Barclays lent a silver lining to this particular cloud. The bank was a far more suitable target for a 'David versus Goliath' campaign than an anonymous airport operator. Stelios led the campaign in person, donning an orange boiler suit and cutting up his personal Barclaycard along with a giant cardboard version during a protest outside the banking giant's Luton branch in June 2000. It was all carefully choreographed, and, predictably enough, the TV cameras and press were in attendance.

The strength of feeling on the issue was evident in a statement released on the airline's website. The wording ran: 'Barclays Bank is obviously not content with closing rural branches, charging for cashpoint withdrawals and granting its fat-cat bosses huge salaries and bonuses. It is now trying to milk easyJet passengers.' This wasn't simply a war of words: by now, easyJet had established a second UK base at Liverpool and was able to increase the pressure by adding new capacity in the north-west, rather than at its spiritual home. It was suggested that if no new deal could be agreed then all future expansion would go to other airports. Upping the stakes further, Stelios lobbied the Secretary of State for Transport, John Prescott, calling for Luton to be regulated in the same way as the other major London airports. Perhaps wisely, the Government kept its head down, saying merely that pricing was a matter between the airport and its customers. The penny had dropped with the politicians that budget airline passengers were becoming a sizeable voting constituency.

Eventually, an agreement of sorts was reached with the owners of Luton airport, but it was far from being an easyJet victory. In February 2001, Barclays cashed out, selling its 65 per cent share in Luton to airport operator TBI for an undisclosed price, said to be in the region of £82 million. On the day of the transfer, as the bank headed for the exit with its bag of cash, easyJet was chasing it down the road to get some of it back. The airline sent Barclays a £700,000 invoice to compensate for what it termed 'a totally unnecessary closure of the airport' following bad weather. According to a statement on easyJet's website, the closure was a result of the bank's 'underinvestment in airport services and poor corporate governance that accompanied its 20 months in control at the airport'.

It would take some time for the dust to finally settle. Despite the change in ownership, bitterness lingered. A 'Barclays Fat Cat Charge' of £4, imposed by easyJet on Luton departing passengers, remained for many months afterwards. The battles with the bank and the airport's management had failed to prevent a steep rise in charges, but it would be untrue to say the campaign had achieved nothing. Once again, Stelios had secured significant PR coverage and reinforced easyJet's positioning as a brand that fights for the interest of customers. The conflict with Luton had spurred expansion at Liverpool and at bases on the continent, where the long-term opportunities for growth were greater. In the final analysis, the bold decision in 1995 to base the airline at Luton had been vindicated. The eventual hike in charges was simply a price for success that would one day have to be paid.

Chapter 11

The geeks shall inherit the earth

When I was school, which admittedly was a long time ago, nerds knew their place. I should know as I was one of them. My secondary education came courtesy of a two thousand pupil comprehensive in a South Wales steel town. If you collected stamps, played chess, showed an interest in computing or suffered from bad eyesight, then you were marked out for bullying. If, like me, you ticked all four boxes, you were a social outcast with the survival prospects of a bunny in a bear pit. At my school, people like me kept their heads down, their mouths shut and counted down the days to summer.

In the eighties, attitudes started to change. When it came to nerds, Bill Gates, the founder of Microsoft, was off the scale. He lived and breathed computers, sounded like Kermit the Frog and had coke-bottle glasses an inch thick. But he was also the richest man on earth and living proof that technology afforded a path to fame and fortune.

Once upon a time, in a land not far away, the airline kingdom was ruled by accountants. This was helpful as it meant executives were aware of exactly how much money they were losing and could prepare their excuses accordingly. The finance department at British Airways was well stocked with over-paid graduates who spent most of their time training for exams the passing of which resulted in their being paid more. Despite marketing staff suffering from bad backs (as a result of too many golf days), the finance team had more comfortable and more expensive chairs because they controlled the purchasing function.

Skip forward a generation to today's leaner and meaner aviation industry. Certain things haven't changed. The finance people remain overpaid, they continue to spend too much time training and persist in performing un-necessary tasks (such as scrutinising the expenses of the marketing team). But the ranks of the bean counters have been thinned, they are occasionally called upon to work after five o'clock and no longer have the best chairs. They have become the *second* most important group of people in the modern airline. If you thought they'd been usurped by the marketing team, then you haven't been paying attention. That Ferrari conspicuously positioned in the company car park belongs not to the airline's chief executive or the finance director and certainly not to its head of marketing. Those are the wheels of the snappily titled chief information officer. Somewhere deep in the bowels of a modern airline you will find its most important group of employees, sipping cans of *Red Bull*, surrounded by pizza boxes and stretching out in the comfortable chairs once occupied by the finance team.

How did this come to pass? Well, it certainly didn't happen overnight. The first technology revolution for airlines came in the late 80s and early 90s. During these years British Airways invested huge sums into computer reservation systems (CRS). This had allowed the airline to get itself in prime position onto the screens of tens of thousands of travel agents around the world. Carriers without their own CRS were obliged to pay a small fee every time one of their flights were sold through a system in which their competitors had an ownership stake. These individual transaction fees added up to hundreds of millions of dollars in revenues every year. BA was a lead player and major investor in *Galileo*, a CRS owned by a consortium of international carriers. American Airlines owned *Sabre*, the largest and most profitable of all the CRS systems. At one point, *Sabre* had become so valuable that the airline's chief executive, Bob Crandall, said his computer reservations system was worth more than the carrier itself. Skilled workers proficient in the arcane computer programming languages that powered these systems were being offered six figure salaries and signing-on fees. Sales and marketing staff looked on jealously as the IT rock stars flashed the cash. Some swallowed their pride and retrained as computer programmers.

There were a few good years until, initially almost imperceptibly, came the first signs of a shift towards direct booking and a weakening of the grip of the CRS companies on global flight distribution. Then along came easyJet cutting out the travel agents altogether, potentially deskilling thousands of trained programmers. It might have been a threat to the march of the nerds, but for one thing. Over the horizon was coming a second revolution, the biggest tsunami of change ever to hit the airline business. It was an unprecedented once-in-a-generation phenomenon called 'the internet', of which more comes later.

It's all very well to talk about technology having the potential to transform an industry, but a company has to be willing to deploy it and to do so at the point of maximum advantage. That requires courage and leadership, ideally from the very top of the organisation. It helped that Stelios was a natural technophile; not that he always wanted the latest and greatest gadget, but more that he had a passion for any application of technology that might aid efficiency in the workplace. At my job interview, he spoke at some length of the paperless office environment he had successfully introduced at his shipping company, Stelmar. He intended to run the same system at easyJet. Under *Keyfile*, every document, fax (and, eventually, email) coming into the airline was optically scanned and categorised according to key words, through which it could be searched for and retrieved. Stelios liked the technology so much that he purchased a stake in the company that owned it.

A key principle behind the *Keyfile* philosophy was that information was of maximum value when shared and accessible by all. Stelios was never one to do things by halves. In our first few months at Luton the paperless office was implemented in its purest form. All employees with a *Keyfile* login had access to every single document held within the airline. This inevitably gave rise to some problems, most notably when it came to finding out how much everyone got paid. It was fascinating being part of what I thought of as a unique experiment in information management and human behaviour. It was probably never sustainable – particularly in light of the raft of data-protection legislation that has emerged in recent years.

There was no more ruthless practitioner of the paperless office environment than Stelios himself. If he spotted paper on your desk, it would be swept unceremoniously into a large blue plastic bin with 'scan everything' written in large letters on the side. As marketing director, I received large quantities of promotional mail, much of it in funny shapes and sizes that weren't easily scanned. But there were to be no exceptions to the rule, and I only learnt my lesson when, for the third time, my desk was swept clear on one of the marauding chairman's paper patrols.

Like most finance directors, easyJet's top money man was, by instinct, wedded to paper. But Nick's desk was spotlessly clear at all times, a tribute to minimalism and making him a gold star pupil. The clues were there if you looked hard enough. Why would Nick whisper in his wife's ear only for her to disappear into the ladies' toilet at frequent intervals? Something was clearly going on, but what could it be? The more observant among us had already rumbled what he was up to. In flagrant violation of the chairman's paperless edict, Nick kept a hidden stash of VAT invoices, insurance certificates and other documents concealed in the ladies' toilets at easyLand. I often wondered what female visitors thought the filing cabinets were doing there. It was the only place in the building where they were safe from Stelios's ongoing crusade to rid the office of paper. The fact that Nick's wife was easyJet's office manager meant that documents could be safely retrieved when required, without questions being asked of Nick's use of the ladies' convenience. Among the management team it became an open secret but Stelios remained in blissful ignorance. He'd shake his head in puzzlement as the management team bantered about being 'flush with cash', making 'payment in lieu' and the need to 'spend a penny'.

While initiatives like the paperless office enhanced productivity, it was the internet that stuck rocket boosters on growth. When the decision was taken to build easyJet's first website in the summer of 1997, no one could have foreseen the extent of the impact it was to have on the airline's future. IT director, Clive Just, and managing director, Ray Webster, were strong advocates for the move online. In contrast, Stelios was initially sceptical, begrudgingly approving a limited budget for the site. 'The internet is for geeks and nerds,' he told us.

We worked initially with *Tableau*, a small Hertfordshire-based marketing agency led by managing director Russell Sheffield. Together we built a site containing information about easyJet's destinations and flight schedules. Customers were not able to transact online, but a special telephone number was prominently displayed. This number appeared nowhere else in easyJet's advertising or other forms of communication. Consequently, we were able to attribute calls coming in on that number as having originated from the website.

The volume of calls resulting from this internet presence was sufficiently large to justify the further investment required to develop an online booking capability. The long march on the road to becoming the self-styled 'web's favourite airline' had begun. In April 1998, easyJet's online booking system went live, with around thirty transactions made on the first day. A couple of months later, when the percentage of business coming in via the internet was in the low single digits, Stelios told me he expected to hit at least fifty per cent by the end of the following year. I thought he was crazy and told him so. On 11th

October 1999, nearly two months early, we hit the impossible target he had set. The reality was that our customers were taking to online booking like a duck takes to water. I had failed to appreciate that the whole transaction process is far easier for the prospective passenger to manage when he or she is doing it themselves. On a computer screen, we could display not just the prices for the first choice of flights but also a number of alternatives. This put the customer firmly in control. They were able to make their own trade-offs between dates and prices and act accordingly. The lengthy waits endured by callers trying to get through to the easyJet telephone centre during busy periods were to become a thing of the past. It was the ultimate win-win, we'd lowered our costs by outsourcing to the customer – and the customer loved it!

In retrospect the chairman's 'crazy' target was comfortably exceeded – not simply because the number of people using the web was taking off, but also because Stelios started taking the tough decisions consistent with the stretching target. A good example was the release of the new season's flight schedule on the internet a week before it was made available via the telephone. The move initially provoked a furious backlash from a segment of our passengers, but we held our nerve and the protests subsided. Another bold decision followed when Stelios elected to go further, offering a £5 discount to passengers booking via the web. This accelerated the migration online. Something remarkable and unprecedented was happening.

A significant milestone was passed in July 2001 when easyJet sold its ten millionth seat through the website, comfortably outstripping its rivals. By the time British Airways arrived at the internet party, easyJet was dancing on the table, belting out some decent tunes and knocking back vodka shots. A major cost benefit of this new method of distribution soon became apparent. While easyJet was experiencing years of double-digit growth, the size of the call centre at easyLand remained static. Without the internet, we would have had to build several additional centres to provide the booking capability that the airline's growth demanded.

The web was opening up new opportunities to tweak British Airways' tail – and, naturally, easyJet took full advantage. In May 1998 following the launch of BA's own budget airline, we ran online competitions to suggest alternative names for the low-cost clone and to predict how much of the £25 million BA had invested would be written off. The competitions attracted tens of thousands of entries, building a valuable customer database, maintaining momentum and raising the profile of our ongoing campaign. We had discovered a powerful and versatile new weapon that allowed us to respond ever more rapidly to market developments and to outwit competitors who were slow to realise the internet's true potential.

We were alert to the danger that this new weapon might one day be turned against us. There had been a famous precedent. In 1996 a disgruntled passenger embarked on a drawn-out campaign of attrition against the airline he believed had wronged him. Jeremy Cooperstock, a University of Toronto student, registered the domain name *untied.com*, which he used to launch a website for the posting of complaints against United Airlines. At its peak the site was said to be receiving between 50,000 and 60,000 visits each month and was described as the world's first internet 'gripe site'. We were wary of falling victim to a similar campaign and as a precautionary measure purchased the internet address *sleazyjet.com*, which was redirected to our own website. It was better to be safe than sorry. We had picked up from airport staff that the term 'sleazyjet' was increasingly used by passengers ranting about flight delays or other airline mishaps.

Looking back, I can honestly say that easyJet had one of the coolest, cleverest and most laid-back IT teams in the airline business. These guys weren't locked away in some windowless basement with just each other and pizza boxes for company. Instead, they were deliberately seated right next to the call centre at the beating heart of the business. Only a pane of glass separated them from a swirling shark tank of commission-hungry telephone sales agents. If easyJet's booking system or the telephones went down, the agents stopped earning and the reaction was instantaneous. On one occasion, I was made aware of a computer problem by the sound of a hundred people simultaneously shouting 'For fucks sake, Trevor, sort it out!' at the tops of their voices. In the first couple of years, when sales agents were paid exclusively on the number of seats sold, you can imagine the pressure that the easyJet IT team was under to get problems fixed quickly!

But although luck and having the right people were undeniably important, in truth it was Stelios's readiness to experiment and his evangelism for technology-driven change that really made the difference. I doubt whether even Stelios could have foreseen the huge role that technology would play in driving down costs, empowering customers and turbo-charging the growth of his airline.

Chapter Twelve

Pricing and promotions

From a marketing perspective, the years either side of the millennium can be viewed as a period of transition: the old media world still wielded significant power, but the internet was starting to make its presence felt. The trick was finding ways to make the old and the new work effectively together. Nowhere was this more apparent than in the area of newspaper promotions. For many years, traditional airlines, British Airways included, had used such promotions as a means of shifting seats that would otherwise go unsold. These seats were heavily discounted and were offered for sale well in advance of the travel period to avoid diluting revenue that would come to the airline anyway. Normally, an additional hurdle was imposed, such as the requirement to collect a set number of tokens printed in the newspaper over a period of time. What easyJet did to the world of newspaper flight promotions was to supersize it, offering large volumes of off-peak seats at rock-bottom prices that made other travel offers look pathetic by comparison.

Promotions were a key weapon in our sales and marketing armoury, but we couldn't run them alone. I approached most of the national papers seeking partnerships. We were agnostic to their political affiliations but some routes were closed off to us. BA had a long-standing relationship with the Mail Group and our approach to their titles was rebuffed in no uncertain terms. The so-called 'quality' papers also initially turned their noses up though they were happy enough to take easyJet's advertising money. To my mind the real prize would be a tie-up with one of the so called 'red-tops' particularly the *Sun* or the *Mirror* who were in the middle of a vicious circulation war. Back then the *Mirror* was edited by a youthful Piers Morgan, a man in the early stages of a rise to media stardom. His counterpart at the *Sun* was Stuart Higgins, a recent replacement for Kelvin Mackenzie, a colourful if controversial figure who'd edited the paper throughout the Thatcher years. Both titles were at the peak of their powers and wary of the risks of partnering with an airline only a couple of years out of the starting blocks.

We put together a great deal to tempt them and in the end it was the *Mirror* who moved first. Their marketing director, Andrew Kitching, called me to say, 'You've got your promotion, don't fuck it up.' I reassured him with platitudes, but privately shared his concerns. Fulfilment was a big risk given the mismatch between the millions of *Mirror* readers and the limited capacity of the easyJet call centre.

The *Mirror* titled our promotion: 'The world's biggest flight offer'. It wasn't the first, or the last, to carry this moniker, but it was a timely reminder of the scale of the venture on which we were embarking.

We prepared for the onslaught as best we could. Telephone lines normally used by administrative staff were redeployed to the call centre. Every seat was occupied. Somehow, we pulled it off. The readers responded positively to the offer and our telephone system just about held up. When the dust had settled we'd managed to shift around 10,000 seats in a couple of days of which I reckoned 90 per cent would otherwise have flown empty. Stelios was pleased with the outcome. When the circulation numbers came in, the newspaper's management were happy too and wanted more. It seemed we had found a solution to the perennial problem of airline distressed inventory. Over the next twelve months we embarked on a series of promotions with both the *Daily Mirror* and its sister title, the *Sunday Mirror*. Each promotion was bigger than the last, eventually culminating in what we hubristically titled 'The mother of all promotions'.

This time, we had overreached ourselves – by now the tabloid circulation battle had reached its zenith and the *Mirror* had backed the flight offer with substantial TV support.

Anticipating strong demand we had contracted to make available 250,000 one-way flights across the network. It was easily the largest promotional allocation of seats easyJet had made in its history. But it wasn't enough. Undeterred by an extended token collection period, a tidal wave of readers hit the easyJet phone lines as soon as they opened.

In a four-day promotional period, a BT contact estimated we were offered over four million calls at a time when we typically had around a hundred telephone staff on duty. I spent much of the four days hiding from John MacLeod, easyJet's call-centre manager and dodging abuse from senior management at Mirror Newspapers. My voicemail was clogged with readers' complaints, and, in a couple of cases, death threats.

Back at easyLand, the excitement had reached fever pitch. Some of the commission-based staff were making upwards of £400 in a single day. The phone lines were so hot you needed an oven glove to pick up the handset. One of our agents told me of the call he'd just taken: 'The guy had been waiting for hours to get through and was gibbering like a madman when he finally spoke to me. He said he wanted to fly to the south of France for a holiday with his girlfriend. I told him the flights to Nice had sold out. Then he said he wanted to fly to Barcelona, and when I told him there was no availability to that city either, he said he wanted to fly to any place at any time. I ended up selling him two seats from Luton to Aberdeen in the middle of February. The next day he called me back and said I'd tricked him into buying something he didn't want, and insisted on a refund.'

Just when it looked like these types of newspaper-fuelled promotions would collapse under the weight of their own success, the internet came riding to the rescue. Insisting upon online booking as a condition of such promotions meant many thousands of transactions could be handled simultaneously. I breathed a sigh of relief: the customer service backlash had been giving me some sleepless nights.

Maximising revenue by matching supply and demand is critical to all airlines but has particular relevance for low-cost carriers. In order to understand how the likes of easyJet and Ryanair can make a profit on a £29 fare to the south of France while BA makes a loss, one needs to appreciate the difference between fixed and marginal costs. The costs associated with carrying an additional passenger from Luton to Nice on an easyJet plane that was, say, already 70% full, were negligible. For a traditional airline, the marginal costs back in the late 90s included a meal or snack, travel-agent commission, reservations-systems costs plus the costs of printing and accounting for the physical ticket. The new breed of budget airlines could avoid all these expenses, allowing them to sell incremental seats for next to nothing. With the extra revenue flowing directly to the bottom line, it was – in theory, at least –

a finance director's dream. Not only that: each incremental passenger, regardless of the price paid to travel, could be sold products and services ranging from car hire and hotels to travel insurance and scratch cards.

It is important to note, however, that the above is very different from saying that an airline can make a profit by flying a full plane load of passengers to the same destination, all paying £29. The viability of the whole model relies on there being a proportion of passengers willing to pay higher fares to travel at the times they want. Business travellers typically fall into this category. Sports fans attending a particular event and families with children tied to school holidays are other examples. Matching supply and demand through variable pricing is known in the airline business as 'yield management'. For the legacy carriers, including British Airways, maximising revenue in this way had become something of a black art. Its high priests were often highly skilled and well-paid mathematicians.

A typical yield management system has behind it a complex series of algorithms. These predict how full a flight is likely to end up, based on analysis of a route's historical performance and current rate of sale. As a brand-new airline easyJet lacked past booking data, which is an important aid to forecasting future sales. Instead we employed a system of guesswork together with trial and error. A visitor to our offices in the early months of 1996 might have found John MacLeod or myself huddled with Stelios over a PC, going through individual flights, which looked to be selling too fast or too slow, and adjusting the pricing accordingly. Such a system was hugely inefficient but just about workable when easyJet operated just a handful of routes. But we were leaving a lot of money on the table. A long-term solution was needed.

This was recognised by revenue-management whizz-kid, John Stephenson, and managing director Ray Webster who'd joined easyJet with a wealth of experience from Air New Zealand. Together, they brought a more rigorous and automated approach to yield management that unlocked significant extra revenue and delivered a marked increase in profitability.

As well as boosting short-term financial performance, there was a longer term objective. Ray could see that for a direct-sell airline, the technology supporting seat booking was of huge strategic importance. The system used by the airline in the late 1990s was shared with other low-cost carriers and this made it difficult for easyJet to extract any long-term advantage. Ray had a good understanding of computing and was a capable coder in his own right. That's a polite way of saying he was a nerd as well as the guy running the airline on a day-to-day basis. Working with the US software company *Bullet Proof Technologies*, Ray led the development of a highly integrated reservation system, which leveraged easyJet's in-house expertise and intellectual property. It proved to be a long lasting and highly beneficial investment.

By today's standards the early attempts to manage pricing look primitive in the extreme. Modern yield management has become highly computerised. Pricing algorithms are the stuff of rocket scientists who sit at the apex of the pyramid in the IT hierarchy. Regulating demand through real-time pricing has had a significant effect on driving up occupancy levels which are far above the levels predicted in the original business plan. The notion of a maximum price band for a fare now looks like an act of supreme naivety as last-minute passengers travelling through necessity are exploited by airlines of all colours. Like it or loathe it, the low-cost business is where you find tooth and claw capitalism at its starkest.

Chapter Thirteen

Smells like team spirit

I've long held that success in any service business depends in large measure on the quality and motivation of the people who work for it, particularly those in customer-facing roles. Testimony to this belief can be found in the focus on employees at Southwest Airlines who proudly state that, in their business, customers come second to staff. These weren't just empty words. Not only was Southwest consistently profitable and the winner of countless customer-service awards, the airline also enjoyed a reputation for having a particularly close-knit and highly motivated workforce.

Southwest's achievement was all the more remarkable given the airline's size, geographic distribution and rapid growth. The journey from struggling start-up to large successful corporation has profound implications for organisational culture. Put simply, the bigger you get the more difficult it becomes to hang onto the team spirit that makes small companies great places to work. In aviation there were examples both good and bad for easyJet to draw on. Defying convention, Southwest had raged against the dying of the light and maintained the kind of culture more often found in a small family-owned business. In marked contrast, I'd seen at first hand the corrosive effects of poor employee relations during my time working in the United States with British Airways in the early 90s. Seared into my memory was an image of union reps walking the floor of BA's North American call centre in Queens, New York. They wore shirts with 'world's greediest airline' emblazoned on the back. Labour disputes were not confined to the airline's ground-based staff. Over an extended period of time, there were a series of disruptive strikes by cabin crew. The resultant delays and cancellations were hugely damaging to British Airway's financial position and its brand.

Southwest place great store by their considered recruitment process. Their philosophy can be summed up in the often quoted mantra 'Hire for attitude, train for skills'. As we kicked off our recruitment drive for call centre staff this was taken very much to heart. Telephone sales techniques could be taught, easyJet was seeking people who displayed energy and enthusiasm. The vacancies were swiftly filled with around sixty applicants for the twenty positions available. As time went on and the date of our first flight got closer, word spread that easyJet was a serious and well-funded venture. It became apparent we'd need to find a way of dealing with the vast numbers of people who wanted to join us.

Back in the mid-90s, Luton was something of an unemployment black spot. Manufacturing had been decimated by the decline in the fortunes of the town's largest employer, car maker Vauxhall. Local people were ever alert to new job opportunities, particularly if the openings were based at the airport. We put out a message on the local radio station inviting applications for positions with easyJet as cabin crew and telesales agents. In the majority of cases no experience was required and full training would be provided. Those interested were invited to come to easyLand on one of a number of open evenings. Ten minutes before the scheduled start of the first such event, I was working at my desk when Anna Zioura called me from reception.

'This is something you've got to see,' she said.

I was greeted by an unexpected scene of almost biblical proportions. Undeterred by falling rain, a queue of over two hundred hopefuls stretched from the front entrance of easyLand, snaking through the car park right up to the perimeter fence. If it wasn't for the absence of complaining children and the smiles on the faces of those standing in line, you might have thought a branch of IKEA had just opened at Luton Airport. We were totally unprepared for such numbers but in true easyJet fashion improvised as best we could. After registering at reception, the candidates were funnelled through a hallway into a small room where Stelios, Dave McCulloch (our Operations Director) and I sat around a large desk. With so many applicants to get through, each 'interview' lasted less than three minutes. We asked them two questions chosen at random from a list of half a dozen and, based on hand signals, indicated to one another whether we felt they should be invited back for a second interview. Stelios was adamant that everyone who'd applied should be seen; 'they've been waiting for hours, plus they're all potential customers,' he pointed out. It was a long, coffee-fuelled evening. By the time the last applicant had gone home, not only was it close to midnight, it was also clear that we wouldn't have a recruitment problem for frontline staff.

At easyJet's next management meeting we brainstormed ideas on how to streamline future recruitment initiatives. I proposed a simple policy. In cases where there were more than a hundred applications for a vacancy, CVs should be divided into two equal piles. One pile would be reviewed in the normal way. The other was to be thrown straight into the bin. Not only would this help to reduce the recruiter's workload, but also meant easyJet could avoid hiring unlucky people. I'm still waiting for the idea to be taken up.

With employee numbers growing, we worked hard to replicate Southwest's successful people-oriented formula. An internal 'culture group' was set up with elected representatives from different departments. Led by newcomer and relentless optimist Chris Goscomb, this team was charged with maintaining a strong company culture as easyJet continued its relentless expansion. Returning from a trip to Dallas, Stelios had brought back with him 250 copies of *Nuts*, the best-selling story of Southwest's success. The books were distributed to the airline's managers and key suppliers; this particular visit had clearly made a big impact on him.

In the months that followed, selected easyJet employees, including myself, were sent off to the US on week-long study tours to watch and learn from Southwest. Rather than shroud their successful people formula in secrecy, they operated an open-door policy to airlines around the world.

My moment of personal epiphany came during a scheduled observation in the shimmering summer heat of New Orleans Louis Armstrong airport. A group of Southwest employees were unloading passenger luggage from the hold of a Boeing 737 when the heavens opened. A clap of thunder heralded the unleashing of a torrential tropical downpour. Steam rose in waves from the hot tarmac but the baggage handlers were undeterred and toiled on through the sauna-like conditions. Despite the impaired visibility and hammering rain you could see them moving in time, grinning defiantly as they belted out a classic Elvis number. It was a revelation. I finally understood the essence of the alchemy powering the airline's success.

We returned to Luton fired-up, invigorated and bursting with ideas to put into action. Southwest had a twenty year head start on easyJet in the low-cost game and we plundered their experience unashamedly. Top of the implementation list was the regular after-work barbecue. Admittedly, the climate in Luton was a few degrees cooler than Dallas or New Orleans, but we improvised by erecting a small marquee in the car park outside easyLand. With food and drink provided by the company, the event was open to all easyJet employees and took place every Friday between 6 and 8 p.m. Stelios would sometimes be found manning the barbecue. Although an enthusiastic chef who looked the part, he wasn't nearly as good at cooking sausages as he was at starting an airline. The occasional undercooked sausage (nicknamed 'the Stelios Special') aside, the barbecues were a big success.

In particular such events brought together administrative staff working out of easyLand and the operational teams who were predominantly airport based. Building bridges between these two key parts of the business was an essential element in easyJet's plan to emulate the achievements of Southwest. The operational personnel, particularly the cabin crew and ground handling staff, interacted directly with travellers on a day-to-day basis and were able to provide invaluable insight and feedback to the sales and marketing team.

Another idea lifted from the Southwest playbook was the practice of getting management and administrative staff to participate in aircraft turnarounds. Mike Coltman led this initiative, exhorting easyLand based staff to sign up for a shift with 'The Hoover brigade'. Mike would stand with a stopwatch at the top of the aircraft steps, while various members of the head office team puffed and panted alongside cabin crew, trying to perform all the cleaning tasks and required checks in the allocated time. It was a chance for operational staff to laugh at the ineptitude of their senior managers and another great way to build bridges.

It's fair to say that not all the ideas we brought back from Southwest were as successful as the Friday barbecue or the Hoover brigade. Among those which definitely failed to translate was the infamous easyJet 'recognition ceremony'. This involved employees who had delivered over and above the call of duty being acknowledged in a ritual during which they were applauded and cheered by the assembled airline staff gathered in a circle around them. It was a proven success at Southwest and had the added virtue of not costing anything. The applause was supposed to last for a minimum of one minute. Never has sixty seconds seemed so interminable. If ever there was anything that highlighted the cultural chasm between the English and their transatlantic cousins, this appalling ritual was it. To be recognised in such a fashion at this much ridiculed event became known as 'getting the clap'. I found it impossible to keep a straight face in such circumstances. In the end, persistent giggling from more juvenile elements in the marketing department led to the recognition ceremony being quietly dropped.

Cultural differences between different nationalities were capable of throwing up the occasional surprise. In the lead-up to the commencement of easyJet's first international service to Amsterdam in the spring of 1996, we carefully considered our options for launching in the Dutch market. For a scheduled airline it's impossible to make a route financially viable without generating traffic from both ends. Could we really launch an unknown direct-sell airline in a foreign market and expect the public to respond in sufficient numbers? No one really knew because it had never been attempted before.

The challenge was daunting, and, perhaps unsurprisingly, we had a temporary wobble in confidence. There was a concern that insufficient Dutch households had access to a credit card and that there might be a cultural resistance to buying over the telephone. This led to Nick and I making a trip to Amsterdam to meet with one of Holland's leading travel agency chains. They had indicated they would be amenable to working on a commission-free basis. Instead easyJet would pay a modest flat-fee for each completed booking. It proved to be a wasted journey; the whole thing had been a set-up. From the moment we walked into the room it was clear the agency had dragged us to their offices just for the pleasure of saying no. We quickly got over the rejection and the resultant clarity was welcome. It was back to the original plan of exclusively direct, telephone-based distribution.

The next big question was how we would handle calls originating from the Netherlands. On paper at least, the most cost-effective system was to centralise all telephone operations in the Luton centre. Our early recruitment efforts suggested we would struggle to find sufficient Dutch speakers who lived within commuting distance of the Bedfordshire airport. Furthermore, at that time we were neither sufficiently well known, nor were we paying enough, to attract applications from further afield. It was time for plan B.

We approached a large call handling centre near Amsterdam, which agreed to field calls from easyJet's Dutch customers. They would charge us a flat-fee every time a one-way flight segment was booked. It was a straightforward arrangement and contracts were swiftly signed. The system worked well enough, but was proving expensive: on average, it cost three times as much to handle a call from a Dutch customer compared with their English counterpart. Then, one day, as part of a routine visit to the Amsterdam telephone centre, I was listening into calls when the penny dropped. The majority of conversations between Dutch agents and Dutch customers were actually taking place in English! Within a few weeks, we had terminated our relationship with our Amsterdam-based partner and were handling calls in English from easyLand. A small team of native speakers were retained in customer service roles. This was because the Dutch people had a tendency to revert to their native language when making a complaint.

In the early years, although easyJet offered no discounted travel to its employees, staff did enjoy a more unusual fringe benefit. The airline was now running regular PR stunts in the UK and overseas, and employees were often able to participate. In October 1998, easyJet organised a famous trip to Brussels where Stelios was to hold a meeting with European Competition officials. We had lodged an official complaint against British Airways, alleging cross-subsidisation of their low-cost airline, Go. As always, we looked at how we could make our point in style and were helped by the development of new techniques that allowed decals to be applied to aircraft hulls. This avoided both the need for painting and the opportunity cost of leaving the aircraft on the ground while the paint dried. It also enabled tactical marketing messages to be displayed on the exteriors of our aircraft at short notice.

We flew out to the Belgian capital on a specially prepared easyJet aircraft with 'Stop BA, Stop Go' writ large on the fuselage. This time, we had over a hundred orange boiler-suited staff, family and friends along for the ride. The visual impact on the streets of Brussels was extraordinary, making for more great media coverage and further building the brand. The European Competition Authorities (ECA) listened politely as Stelios argued his case forcefully in front of them. But he took so long to emerge from their offices that I was forced to phone American Express to negotiate an increase in my card limit to pay the lunch bill for one hundred and fifty hungry people in Brussels. Even though the officials from the ECA decided not to intervene, the event was judged to have been a success. We'd made our point, the trip more than covered its cost in PR terms and the staff and their families had a great day out.

Chapter Fourteen

When shit hits the fan

As anyone who's ever watched the *Airline* series on TV can testify, coping with the unexpected goes with the territory when you're working in an airport environment. Nevertheless, easyJet seemed to get more than its fair share of customer service challenges in its early years. Fog was the F-word that struck terror into our hearts. It took some time for easyJet's planes to be fully equipped and all its pilots trained with 'category three' capability, allowing landing in conditions of poor visibility. Because it was located at the top of a hill, Luton was particularly susceptible to fog. As a result, we were sometimes forced to divert flights to other airports in the Midlands and beyond. I had first-hand experience of the fall-out.

It was in late 1997 and I was travelling back from a trip to Amsterdam. Dense fog shrouded the Luton runway throughout the day and the prognosis for our flight home wasn't good. Before boarding the plane at Schipol, I put in a call to Luton. Douggie McDonald was the acting duty manager at the easyJet call centre. He'd been at the sharp end dealing with aggrieved passengers for most of the day and I could tell from the tone of his voice that we were in trouble. You didn't need to be a fortune teller to work out what happened next. Our flight circled Luton for half an hour, waiting for a gap, but the fog wouldn't clear and the pilot relayed the bad news to those on board - we were diverted to Birmingham. The news was greeted with a chorus of groans and expletives from the passenger cabin along with the usual refrains of 'I'm never flying with easyJet again'. The misery was compounded by a two-hour wait on the ground in Birmingham before the exhausted passengers were decanted into two coaches for the onward journey down the M6 to Luton.

By now it was well past midnight. I settled into my seat hoping to grab a couple of hours' sleep. At that point an overweight, red-faced and manifestly highly stressed man began to pace up and down the aisle of the coach. He was asking for the contact details of passengers who wished to join him in making a formal complaint to easyJet. I didn't like the look of him. He was heavily tattooed with a shaved head and a thick neck of Mike Tyson proportions. His eyes were bulging like a demented frog pumped full of steroids. The stress was clearly not doing his health any good at all. He looked to me like he might only be one hot dog away from a heart attack.

I closed my eyes and feigned sleep as he pushed past my seat. Suddenly there was a triumphant shout from the back of the coach. Waving his mobile phone in the air, the red-faced man's companion announced that he'd spoken to the easyJet call centre and apparently the airline's marketing director was on-board. Underneath my breath I cursed Douggie and my heart rate instantly doubled. Behind their self-appointed leader a lynch mob had formed and the pitchforks were about to come out. For a few seconds time stood still as I grappled with a moral dilemma. The angel on my right shoulder was telling me to stand up, apologise profusely and attempt to reason with the Mike Tyson look-alike who by this point had rolled up his sleeves and was ready for action. The devil on my left whispered convincingly in my ear that the gentleman concerned looked capable of knocking me out with a single punch. For good measure he reminded me I had two young children and insufficient life insurance. I've always possessed a strong survival instinct and at that moment it kicked in.

Opposite me in the aisle sat a nervous-looking middle aged man wearing a sharp suit and sporting a Daffy Duck tie. He was no Don Draper in the style stakes but I figured he looked, to all the world, like a marketing director and shot him an accusatory look. His eyes lit up in alarm; aware that other passengers were also regarding him with suspicion he stood up and announced in a panicked voice, 'It's not me, I'm an accountant!'

Fog wasn't the only weather-related misfortune to befall us. Snow was a four-letter word among easyLand management as well as in the dictionary. Cancelled flights meant lost revenue, extra costs and were guaranteed to put Stelios in a foul temper. Thankfully, instances like the infamous occasion in the late 90s when a freak weather pattern caused it to snow at Luton airport but nowhere else in the country were rare. But dealing with such incidents was toughening us up. We didn't have the customer service resources of larger airlines, and together with other senior managers, I was sometimes thrown into the front line to deal with angry customers facing long delays to their journeys. For those of us who had no background in handling such situations, it was quite an experience.

In the winter of 1996, there was a memorable incident involving a planeload of passengers who had been stranded at Luton by a bout of particularly severe weather. The disgruntled travellers had been informed that they wouldn't be going anywhere until the following day. I was working late in easyLand that evening, when word came in from our handling staff in the terminal that the passengers were on the brink of rioting. It was snowing heavily, so I put on my boots and winter coat and walked the short distance from our offices to the airport terminal to check out the situation for myself. As I walked through the entry doors with my easyJet identity pass around my neck, a couple of hefty policemen who were walking out said, 'Good luck, son'. There was a shout from the crowd and I was immediately engulfed by a sea of complaining passengers. My efforts to placate them failed miserably. Promising to return, I beat a hasty retreat to easyLand from where I phoned Stelios who happened to be at his apartment in Monaco. My instructions were clear: I was told me to call the finance director at his home, get him to come into the office and give each of the stranded customers £100. Nick was unhappy, not with being called into the office so late, but with the idea of giving refunds. His mood worsened when he discovered there weren't enough cheques in the company chequebook to meet the boss's request. Somehow, word had got through to the passengers that their demand for compensation was being met, but I was sure things would turn ugly again if we didn't deliver.

Down the line from Monaco came our revised instructions: if we didn't have enough cheques then we should pay the delayed passengers in cash. I relayed the message to Nick who promptly exploded, 'Where the hell does Stelios think I'm going to get ten grand at this time on a Friday night?' To Nick's credit, he managed to persuade the Thomas Cook bureau de change in the airport terminal to lend us the cash, which we duly stuffed into a briefcase. With the biggest call centre agent I could find standing guard, the passengers formed an orderly queue to collect their £100. At the head of the queue was an elderly vicar. 'Bless you, my son,' he said as I handed over the money.

Stelios certainly enjoyed a good rapport with the airline's frontline staff, but there was more to easyJet's people-orientated culture than the leadership of a charismatic chairman. For me, there was one particular incident that demonstrated more than any other the team spirit of the young airline and our ability to rise to a challenge. It took place in April 1997 when a series of bomb threats resulted in the sudden and indefinite closure of the Luton airport terminal building. Chaos ensued, with passengers turning up for their flights but unable to enter the terminal. Every other airline immediately cancelled all outbound flights; but we saw an opportunity.

As luck would have it, easyLand backed onto one of the airport taxiways and we were given approval to depart passengers from our offices directly onto the planes lined up outside (difficult to imagine in today's security-fixated world). Announcements went out via the travel desks of local radio stations that easyJet would do its best to get all passengers to their destinations. We swung immediately and forcefully into action. Our offices became a hive of activity. It was still easyLand, but like I'd never seen it before or since. The first thing that hit you, even before walking through the doors, was the wall of noise. The cacophony of voices served as advance warning of the chaotic scenes inside. I've only once experienced something similar, at the main train station in Delhi, India. The easyJet offices were thronged with hundreds of milling passengers, the majority with a mobile phone clasped to one ear. The call centre remained in operation throughout, despite the telephone sales people struggling to make themselves heard above the din. They responded by shouting down the phone, which in turn raised the overall noise still further. Desks, chairs and computers had been removed from the large training room, which now resembled a giant *Blue Peter* set. Makeshift, handwritten cardboard signs indicating destinations were fastened with sticking tape above office desks set up as rudimentary check-ins.

Standing on a desk at one end of the room, airport operations head, Ray Kerr, was doing his best to impart some order. He had got hold of a hand-held megaphone through which his booming voice issued boarding announcements for individual flights. Our 'never-say-die' ops manager, Lisa Roblin, and customer services champion, Jane Horton, were in the thick of things, dealing with problems large and small. A customer desk was set up for passengers who'd missed their original flights. Those who had missed flights on other airlines were advised to go outside where it was quieter and call the booking line (the internet was still a year away). There was an hourly rota for cleaning the toilets. Someone even made a dash to the local ASDA supermarket to restock the office vending machines.

Staff not rostered to work on that day heard what was going on and phoned in to help out. In short, everyone pulled together. We were the only airline to operate from Luton and, amazingly, easyJet was able to depart over a thousand passengers who otherwise would have been unable to travel. Thankfully, the spate of bomb threats ended soon after and airport operations returned to normal. No one who played a part in that very special day will ever forget it. The airline's investment in its people and company culture had been repaid handsomely.

Today, with many thousands of staff operating across many different countries and cultures, easyJet faces significant challenges in managing its people – the kind of challenges familiar to many large multinational companies operating in a fast-moving customer service business. The larger and more successful the airline becomes, the more difficult it gets to hang onto that hard-earned orange spirit. Hard, but not impossible. This chapter ends where it began, by paying homage to the people-based achievements of Southwest Airlines. For more than thirty years, through good times and in the face of considerable adversity, they have sustained a philosophy of putting their people first, and reaped the rewards. If easyJet can come anywhere close to emulating them, it will be a remarkable achievement indeed.

Chapter Fifteen

Take me to your leader

Considering the amount of time he has spent in the public eye actively courting publicity for his companies, the Wikipedia entry for Sir Stelios Haji-Ioannou is surprisingly bland. His achievements to date, most notably, of course, the creation of his beloved easyJet, are concisely summarised in stark prose. But when people ask me about the five and a half years I spent working for one of the UK's well-known entrepreneurs, they invariably want to know more about the man himself than the airline that has defined him. Where shall I start?

Stelios was born in Athens, Greece on Valentine's Day 1967. He never told me much about his early life except that he went to school and played football like most kids. Having completed his secondary education, he went on to study Economics at London's LSE before progressing to a Masters in shipping, trade and finance at Cass Business School. After a spell working for Troodos, the shipping company set up by his father, Loucas, he decided to branch out on his own. The first business he established was in the industry he knew best. Using £30m of family money, he set up his own shipping company named Stelmar. In 2001 the business was listed on the New York Stock Exchange and subsequently sold to a competitor for in excess of a billion dollars. But despite this success, shipping was not the arena where he was destined to make his mark.

Stelios's interest in aviation was first sparked when he was approached about buying a stake in a company operating a franchised route between Athens and London. This led to a meeting in 1994 with Richard Branson and although he subsequently decided not to take up a shareholding, the airline business had got him hooked. Rather than investigate opportunities with conventional airlines, Stelios became interested in the new breed of low-cost carriers that were turning North American aviation on its head. Later that year he made a trip to the Boeing offices in Seattle and to the headquarters of Southwest airlines in Dallas. The rest, as they say, is history.

Over the years I've had the opportunity to reflect on the personal qualities of the airline's founder. For me the defining characteristic of the man is willpower. When he decides to do something, Stelios is like a steamroller and pretty much unstoppable. That's how it was with easyJet; he threw himself one hundred per cent into his new venture. There was only one legitimate excuse for failure, and that was customers not wanting to buy what he was selling. It absolutely would not fail for lack of self-belief or effort on his part.

What was he like as a leader? Stelios only knew one way to lead, and that was from the front. The only person he drove harder than his management team was himself. This was no rags-to-riches tale. By most people's standards, Stelios was already hugely wealthy, with fast cars, a powerful speedboat called *Gee Whizz*, and a penthouse apartment in Monaco. Yet, for a while at least, he was prepared to give up this lifestyle to work in a tin shack in Luton, often into the small hours, before heading off to the local Ibis hotel for a few hours' shuteye. As ever, Stelios had an eye for a bargain. When we set up base in Luton, he initially stayed at the three-star Strathmore Thistle Hotel in the town centre, but he had no hesitation in downgrading when he discovered that the two-star Ibis was around £20 a night cheaper.

The airline's founder had none of the airs and graces you might expect from someone born with a silver spoon (more like a platinum ladle) in their mouth. One afternoon, he had the task of showing a small group of important-looking visitors around easyLand. Judging from their tailored suits, silk ties and handmade shoes, they were most likely investment bankers or lawyers. He offered them a drink from the vending machine and, upon opening a can of Diet Coke, sprayed a shower of sticky brown liquid in all directions. Unabashed, Stelios disappeared in the direction of the toilets. Returning with a roll of paper, he got down on his knees and started mopping the floor. The smartly dressed visitors looked at Stelios in disbelief as he pronounced: 'at easyJet, if we make a mess we clean it up ourselves'. The combination of Stelios's 'roll-your-sleeves- up' attitude, his approachability and easy-going manner greatly endeared him to the airline's junior staff, particularly those working in the call centre, some of whom hero-worshipped him.

For the senior management of the airline, particularly those on the start-up team, the relationship with Stelios was fundamentally different. The early growth phase of easyJet was a tough working environment to be in, particularly for those with young families. Like most entrepreneurs starting a new business, Stelios demanded a lot, with managers expected to make substantial personal sacrifices. Holidays were at the then legal minimum of fifteen days per year and leave of more than five days in a row was frowned upon. The workload was unrelenting. When we were in start-up mode, six-day weeks were the norm and our chairman – at the time unburdened by parental responsibilities – led by example.

Of course we all knew that Stelios could be difficult, particularly when he was under pressure. A strong camaraderie developed between members of the start-up team and we supported one another when times were tough. The worst moment came just a few months after launch, when our operations director, Dave McCulloch, died suddenly and unexpectedly, struck down by a particularly aggressive form of cancer. Dave was a true professional. He was much respected in the industry and had a quick, dry wit. He had played a critical role in getting easyJet off the ground, and, if anything, his death brought the core team closer together. There wasn't much time to reflect – we were fighting to establish the airline, and Stelios was pushing us hard.

Remarkably for a man so often in the public eye, Stelios managed to keep his private life out of the media. From the earliest days of easyJet, he maintained a clear distinction between his business and personal affairs, with the two worlds seldom overlapping. One exception was the party he traditionally held at his Monaco apartment during the Formula One Grand Prix. This was one of the few times you got to see Stelios among his friends. Invitations to this particular gathering were much sought after as his apartment overlooked the harbour and afforded spectacular views of the racing circuit. Yet, even at these events, there were few clues to the private side of his life.

Although Stelios could lay claim to being the man who brought low-cost airfares to the British public, there are other pretenders to that particular crown. The original budget airline pioneer had been Sir Freddie Laker, whose transatlantic *Skytrain* had been forced out of business in the early 1980s. I'd first learned about Laker Airways during my student days. A case study of the airline had cropped up as part of my marketing degree. Later, when I went to work for British Airways, Sir Freddie was like the character Lord Voldemort in the Harry Potter series: everyone knew who he was, but his name was never mentioned. In 1997, over breakfast at The Grosvenor hotel near Victoria Station, I finally got to meet the man who'd proved to be such a thorn in the side of my former employer. I'm not sure whether it was Stelios or Sir Freddie who extended the invitation, but they greeted one another like long-lost friends.

As I listened to the two airline pioneers chatting in animated fashion over a full English fry-up, it was apparent that they had much in common. Nevertheless, I was also struck by the contrast between the two men. To my mind, Laker was a laid-back buccaneer from a different age where aviation still carried with it a tinge of romance. Stelios, meanwhile, was very much the hard-nosed calculating businessman: single-minded, totally focussed and hungry for success.

One characteristic the two men shared was a tendency to recourse to law when threatened. Freddie Laker's catchphrase 'sue the bastards' was an expression that Stelios adopted with relish and his penchant for litigation was set to become something of a trademark over the next few years. Indeed, I lost count of the number of legal threats or actions easyJet initiated during my time with the company. In the first hectic few months, it seemed we were in almost daily contact with Hugh O'Donovan, a sharp and witty aviation lawyer and partner in the London law firm *Wilde Sapte*. Hugh not only provided legal counsel but also valuable commercial input that helped easyJet get off the ground.

What initially puzzled me was how often Stelios would request (and pay for) expensive legal advice that he subsequently choose to ignore. It took me a while to realise that commencing proceedings could often be looked upon as a shrewd promotional investment, regardless of the eventual outcome. But it wasn't just business rivals who ended up staring down the barrel of a lawsuit; a number of close advisers and senior employees experienced the legal lash. Even Nick, easyJet's finance director and first-ever employee, would one day fall out with the boss in a dispute that ended in the courtroom.

Of all the airline owners and bosses, the best-known among the public at large remains Sir Richard Branson. By the time easyJet took off, the founder of *Virgin Atlantic* and multiple other ventures was already a household name. His first move into the European low-cost sector came in April 1996 when he bought the Belgian leisure airline EBA and installed Jonathan Ornstein, formerly of US carrier *Continental Express* as chief executive. Based out of Brussels and rebranded as *Virgin*

Express, the airline operated a fleet of Boeing 737s flying mainly to destinations in southern Europe. In its new incarnation the company significantly expanded its scheduled operations, but – following a promising first twelve months – growth suddenly stalled. Some speculated that Brussels was the wrong place to base a start-up; others thought that the Virgin brand didn't sit well with the low-cost sector. In any event, the airline failed to match the dramatic growth of easyJet or Ryanair and was eventually sold and merged with another Brussels-based carrier. Undeterred, Branson made his next low-cost play on the other side of the world. This time round, he was markedly more successful. In 2000, he established *Virgin Blue*, a low-cost carrier that would eventually become Australia's second-largest airline. Yet although he had 'skin in the game', I suspected that it wasn't just the progress of a low-cost competitor that was attracting Branson's interest in easyJet. With his old enemy British Airways involved, he would almost certainly be watching from afar as we slugged it out.

In July 1998 I attended – along with Stelios and James Rothnie, easyJet's Eton-educated PR Head – a televised lecture given by Branson to BBC's *Money Programme* at the corporation's Television Centre in London. The audience had been carefully selected and included a number of well-known entrepreneurs and business leaders. It was more of a retrospective on Branson's many achievements than a hard-hitting Paxman-style interrogation. The founder of the Virgin group sat facing his interviewer on a high chair in the middle of the studio. He had clearly been well prepared by his PR team and had come armed with some memorable quotes that got the audience laughing.

I'd never met the man who BA's former chairman, Lord King, had famously described as 'the grinning pullover', but I was well aware of his reputation and achievements. Stelios, of course, already knew Branson and when filming was over, we adjourned with him to the BBC bar. Several rounds of drinks later, the licence payer's tab ran out and the bar's shutters came down.

The night was still young and at Stelios's instigation we moved on to a Greek restaurant near to Tottenham Court Road. In this particular establishment, customers were allowed to smash plates as long as they paid for what they broke. The shattered crockery would later be swept up and re-fired in a kiln. The evening was a long one: Stelios and Branson seemed to get on like a house on fire. The wine flowed and rude messages directed at British Airways were scrawled on plates with a marker pen before being dashed to the ground. It was childish in the extreme, but highly therapeutic and great fun.

By the end of the evening, the bill for smashed plates was bigger than the one for the actual meal. There was some animated discussion between the two billionaires about who would pick up the tab (I can't recall who actually paid but it certainly wasn't me!). The evening had felt like a celebration and an acknowledgement of easyJet's achievements. It counted for a lot. Richard Branson wasn't just one of the country's most famous entrepreneurs; he was also the man with a reputation for running rings around British Airways. Branson had something else that Stelios coveted: he was widely liked by the British public and consistently featured at the top of lists of most admired businessmen.

Stelios is generally acknowledged to be an accomplished public speaker with an innate ability to handle the most difficult of interviewers. I have long believed that oratory is something you are born with: most airline bosses are, in my opinion, poor speakers, including Sir Richard Branson, who understands the media and communications better than almost anyone. Stelios, however, is a natural. He is never more at home than when in front of an audience or a TV camera. I've lost count of the number of times I've seen easyJet's founder holding an audience in the palm of his hand while displaying a remarkable ability to improvise.

One afternoon, I met Stelios – fresh back in London from a *British Midland* flight – at the QE2 Conference Centre in Westminster five minutes before he was due to deliver a scheduled conference speech. I broke the bad news that I'd forgotten to bring the memory stick containing his PowerPoint presentation, but instead of berating me he simply shrugged. Stepping on to the stage in front of an audience of over five hundred business people he took out of his pocket an apple and a Mars bar that together constituted the 'meal' he'd been given on his flight. 'Will anyone give me a tenner for this rubbish?' he bellowed. 'Because that's what it costs *British Midland* to put it on the plane'. The audience cheered, with some rising to their feet and applauding.

To say that Stelios had an eye for publicity is a bit like saying Leonardo Da Vinci was a dab hand with a pencil. A born communicator, Stelios knew how to work the media to get what he wanted. Journalists loved his accessibility and outspokenness. On any subject relating to aviation, easyJet's chairman could always be relied upon to have an opinion and come up with a good quote. He was certainly not above poking fun at himself if, in doing so, he could be sure of garnering a few column inches. I found his sense of humour to be among his more endearing characteristics. There was a time when, egged on by at least one colleague in the marketing department, I decided to respond to an approach from nearby Whipsnade Zoo. Its fundraising team had sent out mailshots to local companies they believed might be interested in sponsoring some of the zoo's more exotic animals. My interest was drawn immediately to the picture of the chimpanzee on the leaflet. Staring fearlessly into the camera lens as if daring the photographer to take the picture, it was clearly the dominant male. Corporate sponsorship cost just £200 and came with naming rights. I desperately wanted to name the primate, Stelios, but lost my nerve and instead called it 'Daisy', the nickname of one of the media buying team. That might have been that, but one day while randomly inspecting bills online, the chairman discovered the zoo's invoice. He took me into a side room and gave me a bit of a talking to.

'Next time you decide to sponsor a monkey, use your own money,' he said.

'Technically it's an ape not a monkey, and I was intending to call it after you,' I retorted.

He gestured for me to leave the room but I could tell he was smiling.

I thought he might have forgotten the incident. Until, fourteen years later, I participated in London's *Great Gorilla Fun Run*. Together with several hundred other sponsored participants, I ran 7km wearing a monkey suit. All the money raised went to a gorilla charity in Rwanda. Stelios kindly agreed to sponsor me – for the sum of £200!

It was rare for an interviewer to catch Stelios off guard. Indeed, only once do I recall seeing him struggle to answer a journalist's question. The occasion was a scheduled interview with the Scottish *Daily Record* newspaper. The topic of discussion was easyJet's potential initiation of direct services between Glasgow and various European cities. Towards the end of the interview, the journalist threw him the following curved ball: 'so, you started easyJet with a loan of five million pounds from your father, is that right?'

Stelios: 'Yes.'

Reporter: 'Have you paid him back yet?'

In truth, the rest of the Haji-Ioannou clan took little, if any, active part in running the business, even though his brother, Polys, and sister, Clelia, both had substantial shareholdings in the airline. I never met his mother, Nedi, and encountered his father only once when travelling back from Nice on an easyJet flight. It was a chance meeting; I recognised him from photos, though in any event there was a strong familial resemblance. Loucas told me how proud he was of his son's achievements. Clelia I saw a few times after easyJet's launch where she had made a cameo appearance but we never really spoke. Stelios's brother, on the other hand, I met on several occasions, pretty much all football related.

It was obvious to me that we were making headway in our efforts to establish the airline in the minds of the British public. I noticed that when walking down the street with Stelios, people would sometimes stop us and ask for his autograph. It was scarcely surprising when his face was appearing on a regular basis in the national newspapers. The PR stunts were never-ending as we took bigger and bigger risks to corner the headlines. Invariably Stelios led from the front. How far was too far? Well, there was one time where I chickened out big time.

A plan was hatched to drive to Heathrow in a van loaded with a bucket of orange paint, some brushes and a stepladder. The idea was to paint the easyJet telephone number on the side of the thirteen-metre-long scale model of Concorde that once stood outside the road tunnels at the main entrance to Heathrow. Constructed by British Airway's engineering apprentices at some point in the late 80s, it was an impressive symbol of the airline's dominance of the London airport. I undertook a late-night reconnaissance mission. It was well after midnight but there was a steady flow of traffic through the tunnels. The whole area round the Concorde was bathed in bright light. Even pre-9/11, it was a step too far. The world's busiest international airport is not an ideal best place in which to undertake night-time clandestine operations. I have often wondered what might have happened had we actually gone ahead. Would we have made the front pages with the sheer audacity of our stunt? Would we have been arrested and fined? Or might we even have perished, Bonnie and Clyde style, in a hail of bullets at the hands of armed police?

But it wasn't just the marketing of easyJet that attracted Stelios's attention. He seemed to have an interest in almost every part and process within his airline. His grasp of business and finance was exceptional, he clearly 'got' technology and there was no one better at negotiating with suppliers. He had a remarkable ability to simplify problems and possessed a good nose for bullshit. There was no doubt that Stelios was hugely opinionated and, at times, as stubborn as a mule (although he could be moved). If you were trying to convince him about something, the best approach was to stand your ground. He'd look hard for weaknesses in your argument, but if you didn't back down and had a strong case he was prepared to change his mind. The good news was that if you persuaded Stelios, then that was invariably enough for things to start to happen. Decisions could be taken at the speed a start-up needs, to avoid missing opportunities and losing momentum. For those of us who came from a more corporate background, and accustomed to presenting business cases to endless committees, this kind of accelerated decision-making was a refreshing experience.

To some his accumulated wealth has become a defining characteristic. You need only to search on Google for 'the billionaire Stelios Haji-Ioannou' to see this in evidence. The easyJet share price underpins his ranking in *The Sunday Times* Rich List but just how wealthy is he? We are all free to speculate, though the true extent of his net worth has never been disclosed. At its March 2014 peak, easyJet's share price topped £18, valuing his family's stake in the airline at close to £3 billion. Then there are the proceeds of the sale of his former shipping company, Stelmar, the value of the assorted investments in the easy businesses, the revenue stream from the brand license, ongoing dividend payment plus whatever portion of the family fortune that passed down the line on his father's death. It is by any standards a staggering amount of money. In the 2013 television documentary *Flights and Fights*, BBC presenter Charles Miller posed the question: 'Have you made enough money?' Stelios responded by saying, 'I don't know, what's enough'? What indeed?

In concluding, it's simpler, (and from a legal standpoint, safer), to stick to the facts and the most central fact of all is this: without Stelios there would have been no easyJet. How that might have impacted the lives of millions of Europeans is debatable but impossible to quantify. The slack in the system might have been picked up by a foreign airline with a headquarters, jobs and tax domicile outside the UK. The many entrepreneurs and leaders of the country's businesses large and small who've drawn inspiration from the achievements of easyJet's founder might have hesitated before striking out on their own. The start-up team would never have experienced the adrenaline rush of being part of the most successful start-up in the history of UK aviation … and I would never have met my wife Kathrin. An introduction by easyJet's founder in a Luton hotel led, several years later, to a romantic wedding at Ardanaiseig on the banks of Scotland's spectacular Loch Awe.

As a boss, the man was simultaneously dynamic, inspiring, challenging and utterly infuriating. But, at the end of the day, the big decisions always came down to him – and most of the time he called them right. How would I personally sum him up? Once asked in an interview to describe Stelios in a single word, I came up with 'unique' had they asked for three words instead, I would have appended '… thank God'.

Chapter Sixteen

Ryanair

It had come as something of a surprise to discover that easyJet was not the only low-cost airline that had chosen to operate out of Luton. We shared the airport with a feisty Irish carrier offering cheap daily flights to and from Dublin. It was clear from the outset that there was no love lost between us. Every morning their blue and yellow liveried BAC 1-11 jet nosed past easyLand, generating cat-calls and abuse from the building's occupants. I was convinced the pilots deliberately revved the aircraft engines at the point of closest proximity.

The Irish airline had a name that sounded the same when you pronounced it backwards. They called themselves Ryanair and were something of an anomaly in the aviation business. By the time easyJet started-up, they'd been around for ten years, an achievement in itself. Founded by the Ryan family, (no prizes for guessing that one!) the airline began life in July 1985 operating daily flights on a 15-seater Bandeirante aircraft between Waterford and London Gatwick. Within a year they'd graduated to 46-seater turbo props and began their service from Luton to Dublin, taking on both British Airways and Aer Lingus. The launch fare of £99 return was less than half the lowest return fare offered by competitors and triggered what was later claimed to be Europe's first fare war. At some point in 1989, in a moment of madness, possibly following a late-night drinking session involving vodka shots and hallucinogenic substances, Ryanair introduced in-flight meals and a frequent flyer scheme.

Come 1990 the Bandeirante had been retired and Ryanair was operating a combination of BAC 1-11 jets leased from the Romanian airline *Tarom* and ATR turboprops. By now the Irish airline was flying three quarter of a million passengers a year, but the financial losses were stacking up. Hardly surprising since they were fighting a fare war with not one but two much larger airlines, while operating a mixed fleet of expensive aircraft. Financially they were in a tailspin. At some point their investors' patience was guaranteed to run out.

'Commeth the hour, commeth the man.' Enter Michael O'Leary, not so much an airline man as the pantomime villain out of central casting. Based on the reputation that today precedes him, you might have imagined he was spawned by an evil wizard in the toxic filth of a deep, dark orc-infested cave. The reality is much more mundane. Born one of six children and brought up on a farm in Kenturk, County Cork, O'Leary trained as an accountant and spent time working for the blue-chip firm KPMG. His talents were recognised by Tony Ryan who took him on as a personal tax advisor. O'Leary's initial advice regarding Ryanair was that the loss-making Irish airline should be shut down. Undeterred, Ryan appointed his protégé to the top job giving him a free hand in turning the business around. A visit to Southwest in Texas and in particular a meeting with Herb Kelleher proved something of an epiphany for O'Leary who set about a root and branch reform of the Irish carrier.

Backed by an additional £20m in investment from the Ryan family, the airline transitioned rapidly to the Southwest operating model. The ATR turboprops were deemed surplus to requirements. Instead, they opted for a single aircraft type equipped with modern fuel efficient jet engines. The new look Ryanair would in future only fly routes that were capable of supporting high frequency services at low fares. The airline's home base was relocated from Luton to Stansted, in-flight meals and frequent flyer programme were banished never to return. With a revamped and highly scalable business model in place Ryanair embarked on a thirty year journey of growth and profitability. It has never looked back.

Some people consider it strange that Europe's two largest and most successful low-cost airlines have, for much of their respective histories, avoided direct head-to-head competition.

For the first few years following easyJet's launch, minor skirmishing on the Glasgow route aside, the low-cost rivals took growth paths that were largely divergent. Of course we shared a common foe in the shape of British Airways and for as long as the two carriers remained relatively small it might be argued there was little sense in wasting energy on destroying one another. But there was another explanation as to why we so rarely crossed swords.

Whilst easyJet focussed for the most part on growing traffic to major cities and population centres, Ryanair adopted a fundamentally different approach to route selection. Their strategy was to fly to secondary airports, often in places you'd never heard of, that offered rock-bottom landing fees. These included Hahn and Torp, located 110km and 118km respectively from the cities of Frankfurt and Oslo they allegedly served. In 2002 Britain's Consumer Association claimed the airline's advertising had led customers to think they were flying to the Danish capital of Copenhagen when they actually landed at Malmo, an airport located in Southern Sweden.

Ryanair's route map, apart from looking as if it had been drawn by a six year old, portrayed an eclectic collection of seemingly random European towns and cities the majority of which, despite my having achieved a grade B in GCSE Geography, were unknown to me. I evolved a theory that O'Leary and his route-planning manager had indulged in a late-night drinking game involving a bottle of high-strength vodka, a set of darts and a map of Europe pinned to the wall. Wherever a dart landed, the nearest airport was added to the destination list, with the proviso that neither of them had heard of it. An easyJet advertising campaign highlighted the obscurity of Ryanair's chosen landing points, employing the messaging "We fly you to an airport, not an airfield". It was a good line but in truth passengers appeared not to care. They were prepared to go significantly out of their way in order to access the lowest fares. Regardless of how the list of routes had evolved, evidence suggested their strategy worked.

Safety and punctuality aside, Ryanair took cost-cutting to new levels by looking at every opportunity to lower prices. Their obsession with cost control made easyJet look profligate in comparison. Staff were encouraged to follow O'Leary's example and steal pens from hotels, though the allegation they were banned from charging their mobile phones using the company electricity turned out to be an urban myth. The Irish airline showed that it could play the public relations game, too. It issued headline-grabbing announcements on a range of controversial proposals including extra charges for overweight customers, fees to use the toilets and even outlined ideas for an aircraft that allowed standing-room only. None of these initiatives have yet come to pass, but invariably they have generated substantial press coverage for Ryanair; reinforcing its reputation as a cost cutter *par excellence*.

While squeezing costs was a central plank of the Irish carrier's business model, it was accompanied by the ruthless pursuit of ancillary revenues. This was a dark art that Ryanair not only mastered but took to new levels. It was all about having the lowest base fare in the market and then building the revenue back up through the sale of 'stuff'. If you were a monk: travelling alone, lacking a driving license, undertaking a fast, who carried your worldly possessions in a handkerchief and were happy to sleep under a tree, then you stood an excellent chance of Ryanair not selling you anything. It would help if you'd also taken a vow of silence. Even then they'd likely wake you up during the flight and try to flog you a scratch-card using sign language.

Like Stelios, O'Leary was quick-thinking, opinionated and ambitious – but that was where the similarities ended. It was true that Stelios could occasionally be quick-tempered with his management team and suppliers, but to employees in general and customers in particular he was polite and charming. I rarely, if ever, heard him swear. In contrast, O'Leary appeared not to care whom he upset. He spoke forcefully and directly to the media, peppering his pronouncements and press conferences with bad language. In a 2019 TV documentary for Channel 5 the airline's former commercial director Tim Jeans described what it was like to be involved in a Ryanair management meeting with O'Leary present. He compared the experience to a scene from a wildlife film where a crocodile emerges without warning from a watering hole and seizes a wildebeest in its jaws.

Journalists could always rely on him for a good story and memorable one-liners. Among the more colourful quotes ascribed to O'Leary by *The Guardian* in an article dated 8th November 2013 is his infamous pronouncement: "You're not getting a refund so fuck off. We don't want to hear your sob stories. What part of 'no refund' don't you understand?"

Unlike their orange rival, Ryanair had an established history of selling through travel agents. They continued to do so for several years, even after their Damascene moment of conversion to the Southwest operating model. It wasn't until 2001, six years after the launch of easyJet that they finally severed their agency links, declaring in a letter they would no longer sell through the trade. Overnight the name of Ryanair's boss was scribbled off travel agents' Christmas card lists throughout the UK and Ireland. I doubt he lost much sleep over the decision. The same *Guardian* article quoted O'Leary as saying "Screw the travel agents. Take the fuckers out and shoot them. What have they done for passengers over the years"?

To my eternal regret, I wasn't at easyJet in 2003 to witness one of the most famous Ryanair stunts. In a scene straight out of the pages of *Boy's Own*, Michael O'Leary, dressed in battle fatigues, drove a Sherman tank belching smoke towards Luton airport on a mission to 'liberate the public from easyJet's high fares'. The tank's ultimate objective was the easyJet offices, but its progress was halted by airport security halfway up the hill leading to easyLand. Confined to the car park of the Holiday Inn Hotel, O'Leary and supporting Ryanair staff chanted slogans and sang uncomplimentary songs about their orange rival while the theme tune from *The A-Team* blared from loudspeakers.

It was clear there was no love lost between the two men. The closest O'Leary ever got to ever paying a compliment to his Greek rival was to say: 'He's the son of a billionaire. He could have been a rich tosser but at least he did something and set up an airline.' Verbal sniping from both sides flared up from time to time but red lines remained uncrossed.

Then in 2010 came the flashpoint. Ryanair ran an advertisement in the *Daily Telegraph* and *Guardian* newspapers picturing Stelios with an elongated nose reminiscent of the Disney character Pinocchio. The copy referred to easyJet's founder as 'Mr Late Again' and called on him to 'stop hiding the truth' about the airline's on-time performance. It was not a smart move.

Predictably, Stelios went to his lawyers, the London firm *Schillings*, who issued a letter accusing the Irish carrier of making 'baseless and defamatory statements about him'. Instead of backing down, the move prompted further insults from O'Leary. As an alternative to a legal battle, the Irishman threw down a series of challenges to settle the dispute, including a *Chariots of Fire*-style race around Trafalgar Square. When this was rejected, O'Leary proposed a Sumo-wrestling bout, declaring, 'as long as he provides the nappies, bring it on'. But it was Stelios who emerged victorious when Ryanair was forced to apologise and pay damages of £50,100 plus the legal costs of easyJet's founder.

It would have required little effort to fill out this chapter by drawing on the abundant quotations attributed to the Ryanair boss. His outspoken public utterances have led to him becoming a caricature of himself. But should he be defined by them? Few successful people are as one-dimensional as the evidence might suggest. People who know Michael O'Leary privately, describe him as charming and generous. I met him just once, at easyLand with Stelios back in the late 90s. I don't recall what it was regarding and very much doubt he remembers me. Our receptionist Becky told me he was a polite man who'd waited patiently and asked her what it was like to work at easyJet.

Under his leadership Ryanair has metamorphosed from a struggling Irish carrier into one of the world's largest and most profitable airlines. His critics are able to call on an arsenal of ammunition, yet they cannot detract from the scale of his achievement. The airline he turned around has enabled hundreds of millions of people to access Europe's skies. I'll leave the final word to the *Economist* magazine, which once concluded an analysis of the company by saying that Ryanair has managed to be both utterly successful and absolutely disliked.

Chapter Seventeen

Growing pains

By late November 1995, with the launch behind us and our two aircraft shuttling up and down between Scotland and Luton, Stelios convened a meeting to take stock. From a marketing perspective it was a case of 'so far, so good'. The airline continued to attract significant media coverage contributing to a growing awareness of the brand amongst our target audience. The plan was to keep easyJet in the headlines for as long as possible before the public's interest started to wane. The easiest way to achieve this was to antagonise British Airways at every possible opportunity.

For two long weeks, despite our continued attempts to provoke them, BA steadfastly refused to publicly acknowledge easyJet's existence. We had thrown down the gauntlet but our opponent was not inclined to pick it up. Frustration started to creep in. We badly needed a fight if we were to generate the awareness that would keep the phones ringing and our planes full.

Then, suddenly and surprisingly, British Airways succumbed to its basic instincts. Having said that easyJet's fares were unsustainable, it countered our £29 one-way prices with a £58 return fare of its own, albeit requiring an overnight stay and with limited availability. Glasgow and Edinburgh began to appear regularly as featured destinations in BA's tactical promotion of their so-called 'World Offers'. The company vehemently denied this was designed to dislodge the foothold easyJet had established on these routes.

Stelios decided that the best form of defence was to attack. We scrapped the higher fare bands altogether and took the decision to offer all unsold seats at our lowest fare of £29 for travel up to Christmas. This meant forgoing significant amounts of revenue, but it made for a simpler marketing proposition and was impossible for British Airways to match. Sales ticked up, but it wasn't enough. There was still plenty of availability, particularly on our mid-week flights.

For the first time since the launch, I was nervous. For me, this was the moment of truth. If we couldn't fill our planes even when we offered all our seats at £29, how would we ever fill them at the higher prices we needed in order to become profitable? Stelios decided to raise the stakes once more.

Our marketing plans and budgets were thrown out of the window. We scrambled to buy almost every advertising space we could find. Full-page advertisements in the London *Evening*

Standard and the Scottish press, wall-to-wall radio and, incredibly, even a TV advertising campaign all cobbled together in a matter of days. With advertising slots difficult to obtain at short notice in a tight, pre-Christmas market, we were struggling to spend the money. Mike Hellens, the MD of our media-buying agency, Matters Media, was called into the offices to explain why we were having problems getting the level of coverage we wanted. In no uncertain terms, he was told to find a way of spending a million pounds. Otherwise, he'd be fired. Mike shrugged. He was on commission and stood to make a substantial sum from the increased expenditure. Of course it could be done, but to spend that kind of money in a short period of time, we'd need to get on television. Without any hesitation, Stelios approved. This was the kind of big, bold, getting-on-the-front-foot decision he relished.

Conventional wisdom dictates that it takes at least a month to make a television ad. Many creative agencies will want as much as three months; allowing time for research as well as creative development and execution. Somehow, we managed it in less than a week. The finished product was awful – so awful, it reminded me of one of the cheap local curry house promotions you see if you arrive early to watch a movie at the cinema. The hastily produced advertisement featured a hand holding a model easyJet plane aloft. In the background a voice proclaimed excitedly, 'Scotland for £29 with easyJet. Call direct, Book direct, Fly Direct.' The production quality was so poor that people assumed we'd deliberately made it that way to underline the fact easyJet didn't waste customers' money.

During this phase of the airline's growth, Stelios was like a man possessed and the atmosphere at easyLand was electric. At one stage, we were working six or seven days a week, our days peppered with crisis meetings and calls to action. I had one eye constantly on what Stelios had nicknamed 'the till', a computer directly linked to easyJet's booking system. The screen displayed a constantly updating picture of what we'd sold so far that day. When the boss was out of the office, every phone call he made to me was prefaced with the words 'what's the till?' And if he didn't like the number I gave him, this was swiftly followed up with '… and what are you doing about it?' In Stelios's eyes there were few greater sins than failing to take immediate action in the face of an emerging problem.

Starting a business doesn't generally go hand in hand with healthy living. As long working days, poor eating habits and lack of exercise began to take their toll, easyJet's management team and its chairman started to pile on the pounds. If you didn't like fast food or curry, then Luton was a culinary desert. There were no healthy eating options within a five-mile radius of the airport, let alone within walking distance of the terminal. In the airline's start-up phase, one of the few things growing faster than easyJet's advertising spend were the ballooning waistlines of a management team subsisting on cold pizza, Kentucky Fried Chicken and bucket-sized cups of Coca Cola. The only exercise many of us were getting was the five-minute walk, or rather waddle, between easyLand and the airport terminal building to restock food supplies. Stress and long hours began to take its toll on personal relationships. It was relentless. For week after week the advertising tap was kept open and the marketing department worked late into the night, as BA and easyJet went eyeball-to-eyeball. We were on the ropes and I was unsure how long our small team could keep up the pace. It felt that our resolve might crack at any moment.

British Airways blinked first. It seemed they had got the message: Stelios had deep pockets and he wasn't going to be bullied out of the market. We'd taken our opponent's best shots and were still standing. Our adversary throttled back on its discounted promotion of the Scottish routes. I breathed a sigh of relief and allowed myself a day off. Defying the predictions of many within the industry, easyJet had made it to Christmas and, true to form, we celebrated with a big party.

The New Year saw easyJet opening up another front in the war against British Airways. Work got underway in preparation for the launch of services between Luton and Aberdeen. The route between London and Scotland's oil capital was known to be a phenomenal money spinner for the UK flag carrier. It held the distinction of having the highest proportion of British

Airways Gold Card holders anywhere on its global network. Stelios wanted a piece of the action.

The previous year, BA had successfully seen off a challenge from a little known start-up airline called *Aberdeen London Express*, (nicknamed Alex by its passengers and staff.) It was a noble effort. They offered passengers a fare of £60 one way between Aberdeen and Stansted but were significantly under-capitalised and didn't have a snowball's chance in hell of making money. A few months after the demise of his airline, the founder of Alex, Dr Robert Perryment, paid a visit to easyLand. I remember him as being polite, erudite and intellectual. He gave a thoughtful account of how the battle with British Airways had unfolded and the mistakes he believed had been made. To my mind what had transpired was blindingly obvious and entirely predictable. Perryment had ill-advisedly gotten into a street fight with the biggest kid on the block. He had chosen to fight in accordance with the Marquis of Queensbury rules, rather than throwing sand in their eyes and kicking them in the balls. The outcome would have been the same but they might have lasted a bit longer. On reflection I considered how Alex might actually have done easyJet a favour by luring our enemy into a false sense of complacency. Having ruthlessly dispatched the *Aberdeen London Express*, BA was – I suspect – anticipating that it would have little difficulty seeing off this latest interloper's attempt to encroach on their goldmine.

Making an impact at the Aberdeen end of the route was crucial in easyJet's efforts to establish its brand and build awareness. BA appeared to have a stranglehold on advertising opportunities across the city. The two dominant local newspapers, the *Press & Journal* and the *Aberdeen Evening Express*, were owned by the same company, *Northcliffe*, and I arranged to meet them. The proposed advertising rates were ridiculously expensive considering these were regional titles with small circulations. For the first time in my career I'd met an advertising sales manager who simply wasn't prepared to negotiate. Take it or leave it was the only deal on the table and by the look on his face he wasn't bothered if easyJet walked away. I was worried: we were running out of time and options, the load factor (percentage of seats filled) wasn't where we needed it to be. It was time for a change of tactics.

After careful planning and an element of subterfuge, we secured two key poster advertising sites within the Aberdeen airport terminal building. The chosen locations were strategically positioned. One was close to the British Airways check-in desks; the other was above the luggage carousel from which passengers collected their bags. Our booking of the sites was viewed with some trepidation by those responsible for granting advertising copy clearance at the airport, so much so that I received a phone call warning me that easyJet's poster designs would be subject to close scrutiny prior to approval. It was made crystal clear that even the mildest attack on British Airways would not be tolerated.

Sensing an opportunity, we drew up the most outrageous copy we could think of – a design with the tagline 'Beware! Thieves operate in this airport' written in BA's corporate colours and submitted for the site above the British Airways check-in desk. The anticipated rejection duly arrived in the shape of a terse fax, triggering a strategic leak to the media and a sensationalist storyline in the local press. 'New airline's adverts banned' was the headline in the *Aberdeen Evening Express*. We cancelled our poster site bookings and secured a full refund, the coverage had cost us nothing. As we celebrated this latest PR coup, reports came through that advance sales on the route had started to rise. On 26th January 1996, with snow falling and a biting wind to greet the passengers, easyJet's first flight from Luton touched down at Aberdeen airport. Once again, it was full.

Despite this early success, it proved hard work establishing ourselves on the London to Aberdeen route. The initial euphoria passed, BA lowered their prices and easyJet's load factors began to dip. I'd been told that there was always a price at which you could fill any plane on any route. That may have been true, but in the case of Aberdeen in February the price required to fill the plane started with a minus sign – and we weren't willing to pay people to fly!

The problem was the business travellers, or, to be more precise, the lack thereof. Based on sophisticated passenger profile analysis (otherwise known as counting the people lining up at BA's check-in wearing suits), we knew we had some, but not nearly enough. From an early stage, easyJet's natural constituency of small- and medium-sized companies had come across in large numbers. Often, these were the people paying out of their own pockets or working for companies operating on tight margins that watched the pennies. Their custom was appreciated, but it wasn't enough to fill easyJet's planes. The long term viability of the route hinged on our ability to make inroads into the big oil companies like *BP*, *Exxon* and *Shell* that accounted for the bulk of regular traffic. The oil giants' employees booked mainly through large business travel agents such as *Hogg Robinson* and *American Express*, who in those days wouldn't touch easyJet with a bargepole. The underlying problem, however, was the fact that a significant proportion of the travellers between London and Aberdeen were enrolled in British Airway's reward scheme. It was called *Air Miles* and was considered the crack cocaine of frequent-flyer programmes.

In December 1996 in an effort to get back on the front foot, we prepared another salvo for British Airways. It took the shape of a strident advertising and PR campaign attacking airline loyalty schemes in general and BA's air miles scheme in particular. Stelios took the position that frequent-flyer miles were tantamount to bribery. Points were awarded disproportionately for the most expensive fares and, therefore, incentivised corporate travellers to spend more of their company's money. His strength of feeling on this issue was evidenced by the fact that it became expressly prohibited for easyJet's staff to collect air miles when travelling on company business.

In need of another attention-grabbing stunt to build momentum behind our anti-air miles campaign, we came up with a novel idea: for passengers travelling on this route only, easyJet would offer its own 'bribe'. Anyone who booked the most expensive easyJet fare of £69 one way would receive a free bottle of whisky. Having announced the promotion, we needed to lay our hands on five hundred bottles of cheap scotch. Time was short. We went out looking for the best deal we could find. Any significant purchase at easyJet required a competitive tender with offers from at least three suppliers. In this case the winning bid was submitted by a 'Del-Boy' character whose price was considerably below the two other offers. At the time I wondered how he'd been able to undercut them by such a margin. When I opened the first box to arrive at easyLand, the answer immediately became apparent. The bottles were half the standard size. They contained an unbranded golden liquid that smelled more like cheap aftershave than the product of a Highland distillery. In the line of duty, I sampled the contents myself and can testify that we'd got what we paid for. I expected a ticking off but Stelios found the episode amusing and said we should learn from the experience.

The product on offer didn't go down too well with some of the passengers standing in line at the Aberdeen sales desk to collect their bribe. British Airways passengers had refined palates developed over years of sampling fine wines and few of them came back for a second bottle. A ground handling agent told me that during this time it was common to find rejected bottles of whisky littering the departure area.

Air miles remained muted throughout our campaign. Unsurprisingly the company had no intention of being drawn into a debate about the morality of frequent flyer schemes. Ironically, however, an advert we published in the *Glasgow Herald* did provoke a response though it had been aimed at a different target. For the first time, we crossed swords in an advertising dispute with Ryanair who had recently begun operating to Prestwick airport in Ayrshire.

The destination was promoted by Ryanair as 'Glasgow Prestwick', even though Prestwick is nearly forty miles from the Scottish city. Our offending advert was entitled 'Ayr Miles', with the sub copy 'easyJet fly from Glasgow International not Prestwick'. We were a little hypocritical to complain since we were marketing Luton as 'London Luton', but that didn't stop us. The anticipated reaction came not from Ryanair, who wisely stayed silent, but from *Air miles* itself, in the form of a solicitor's letter telling us our use of the expression 'Ayr Miles' was a phonetic infringement of its intellectual property. Stelios's predictable reaction upon seeing this legal warning was to tell me to run the advertisement again.

It would have been quite something if easyJet had succeeded in its mission to eliminate frequent-flier programmes or, at the very least, to bring wholesale changes to the way in which they operate. Perhaps we should not be too surprised that the majority of air travellers seem to draw a distinction between how they spend their own money and that of their companies. Today, frequent flyer programmes remain a key weapon in the armoury of the legacy airlines as they defend their diminished but still significant share of the European business travel market against the low-cost horde. The prohibition on collecting of frequent flyer miles while travelling on company business remains etched into easyGroup employment contracts.

With easyJet now flying to Scotland's three largest cities, opportunities to add further destinations north of the border were decidedly limited. The only other commercial airport capable of handling large passenger jets was Inverness, gateway to the Highlands. During my time as a graduate trainee at British Airways, I'd been asked to write a report on the airline's importance to remote communities. After spending a week flying round the Highlands and Islands, I'd fallen in love with the spectacular scenery that part of Scotland had to offer. I was convinced that the market had significant growth potential.

Our timing was impeccable. The 1995 Oscar-winning movie *Braveheart* had given a significant boost to tourism. Furthermore the city of Inverness was on the cusp of significant economic and population growth. One morning in late spring 1996, I took the early flight to Aberdeen for a brief meeting aimed at strengthening our local marketing efforts. Instead of flying back to Luton, I hired a car and set off to Inverness. A meeting had been arranged with Bob Macleod, the Highland airport's managing director. We'd already established there would be no significant discount on easyJet's landing fees, but I was hopeful of some marketing support to help promote the route. The formal rituals of hospitality were observed, but the reception was decidedly lukewarm. I was offered a cup of tea (also lukewarm) but without the accompanying piece of shortbread or Tunnock's teacake I'd been hoping for. It summed up the deal on offer. Within five minutes Bob was looking at this watch, within ten I was being shown the door. A faint smell of sulphur lingered in the air; had the British Airways representative been in ahead of me?

I arrived back at Luton empty-handed but undeterred. The absence of financial incentives meant this was a far from clear-cut decision for easyJet. Inverness was twenty minutes' flying time further north than either Glasgow or Edinburgh and, consequently, more expensive. Despite some misgivings, I lobbied hard and was absolutely delighted to be given the green light.

In comparison with Glasgow and Edinburgh the city of Inverness was a tiddler. The city's wider catchment area consisted largely of crofters and sheep. With just one flight a day timed in the early afternoon, there was no prospect of capturing passengers travelling down to London for a day's business. To a large extent we would be dependent on highly seasonal tourist traffic to fill our aircraft. This route would provide a real test of easyJet's ability to compete. We racked our brains in the search for cost-effective opportunities to provoke British Airways and grab the headlines. One particular stunt involved Stelios scuba diving in Loch Ness looking for the BA low fare ('everyone's heard of it, but no proof of existence has been found'). The weather forecast was appalling and I feared the murky waters of the loch might conceal a BA frogman armed with a harpoon gun. The photo opportunity was called off. It didn't matter. I was starting to learn that you didn't always have to go through with a stunt in order to get publicity out of the original idea.

We worked closely with the Scottish Tourist Board to promote the appeal of the Highlands to Londoners. They invested £400,000 on a campaign of poster advertising at London's mainline and underground station featuring easyJet as a promotional partner. The deal was sealed with a few drams of good whisky and some jokes at BA's expense.

With the benefit of hindsight I can see that my heart was guiding my head. I was spending a disproportionate amount of time developing marketing campaigns for a single daily flight on a secondary route when my attention should have been focused on easyJet's critical push into Europe. But I also believed that a service linking Inverness and Luton would be good for the airline, good for the regional economy and good for travellers to and from this part of Scotland.

Consequently no one was happier than me when in November 1996 the first easyJet flight touched down at a windswept Dalcross airport. Proudly emblazoned on the hull was a huge decal of the Loch Ness monster. After a slow start (believe me, the Highlands are a tough sell in winter!), Inverness turned a corner: load factors were low compared with the other Scottish destinations, but the revenues were higher than anticipated.

Importantly, we'd proved that the easyJet formula could work for a leisure-dominated route. With four Scottish destinations under our belt in the first twelve months of operation, we published an orange credit-card-sized airline timetable, recouping the printing costs by selling advertising on the back. It was a small token of our success, but somehow it felt like we'd passed another milestone.

Chapter Eighteen

The empire strikes back

In November 1996, with easyJet established on the Anglo-Scottish routes and flushed with success from its first raids into Europe, British Airways made a sudden and unexpected approach. Their chief executive, Bob Ayling, invited Stelios to meet at the company's Hatton Cross offices in West London, telling him: 'I think you've cracked it'. This was unexpected in the extreme. It was as if Darth Vader had invited Luke Skywalker round to the Death Star for a cup of tea and a ginger biscuit. Had the BA boss announced Vader style 'I am your father' it might have come as less of a surprise than the news that our mortal enemy was contemplating buying a stake in easyJet.

Discussions continued through the winter of 1996 before BA, somewhat feebly, informed us the negotiations were to be broken off. They had apparently formed a view that the deal was unlikely to secure regulatory approval. Stelios's fury at this rebuttal was accentuated when, in October 1997, British

Airways announced its intention to launch its own low-cost airline. Initially it was called 'Go fly', before being shortened to 'Go'. Within hours of learning of BA's decision, Stelios was on the phone to the lawyers, reportedly arguing, 'There's no point in waiting until you're out of business. Sue and sue early.' Our founder believed BA had tricked him by expressing interest in investing in his airline with the sole objective of getting close to our secrets. The acquired knowledge had then been applied in the creation of Go, which he described as a photocopy of the easyJet business plan. Needless to say, British Airways denied any duplicity, but it was a key turning point – both for easyJet and its chairman. From that point on, Stelios redoubled his efforts, focussing all his energy on winning a war that had now become personal.

Our public stance was that BA was incapable of running a low-cost airline. Indeed, history suggests that budget airlines started by conventional carriers are even more prone to failure than standalone start-ups. But, for all our outward bravado, I personally believed that Go would prove to be a more serious competitor than some of my colleagues imagined. I remembered Barbara Cassani, Go's Chief Executive, from my days as a graduate trainee with British Airways back in 1990. Bright, articulate and sassy, she stood out in a crowd of middle-aged men in grey suits. Cassani was seen as a real high flier with potential for the very top, and this was to be her chance for glory. What's more, she had assembled a good team of people around her, including operations supremo Ed Winter, and Jane Willacy, an immensely capable individual with whom I'd previously worked at BA and admired greatly.

Initially, the plan had been to concentrate our marketing fire on BA, who Stelios believed was pulling the strings, rather than 'Go' itself. This was a deliberate move: we wanted to avoid creating awareness for our new competitor, and it also made for better PR. 'David versus the slightly bigger boy from the next village' is unlikely to hit the headlines, but 'David versus Goliath' is always going to make for a good story. This would be a war waged in full view of the public.

Stelios wasted no time in rolling out the big guns. Full-page advertisements were placed in a number of the national newspapers, using the slightly contrived metaphor of Beauty and the Beast. Barbara Cassani and BA Chief Executive, Robert Ayling, were respectively depicted in the two roles. The ads questioned the motives of British Airways in starting a low-cost airline. We contended that the sole purpose of setting up Go was to put its orange rival out of business, before raising fares again. Like most of easyJet's tactical campaigns, it was put together at lightning speed – and was a lot of fun to work on. We quickly found an attractive picture of the Go chief executive and searched hard for the most unflattering image of Ayling we could find; ideally we were after a shot that made him look aggressive, bug-eyed and threatening. It proved more difficult than anticipated. Instead of a scar-faced, power-crazed Bond villain with a cat on his lap, the British Airways boss resembled a game-show host from a minor US cable channel. He wore sharp suits, had expensive teeth and his hair was immaculately coiffured.

The time had come to give the hornets' nest another hefty kick. We knew there had been opposition to Go's launch from elements within BA's own ranks. This faction believed (rightly in my view) that the move would damage the airline's premium brand positioning. To exploit these internal tensions and to highlight the brand inconsistency, the ads included a drawing of the Concorde aircraft with the words 'cheapo airline' scribbled on the side. We were now spending serious advertising money: the larger spreads in the national dailies and the *Economist* cost upwards of £10,000, but this was a crucial roll of the dice.

With the assistance of advertising salespeople whispering in the ears of their editorial colleagues, the media were starting to swing behind easyJet. On 01st November 1997 an opinion piece appeared in the *Financial Times* stating that regulators would need to watch British Airways like hawks. In a similar vein, an article in the *Daily Telegraph* suggested that BA launching a low-cost airline would result in the disappearance of independent airlines and an increase in prices.

Aside from the media, our other key battleground was to be the courts. Stelios wanted the best legal brains money could buy working on the case. Our QC was to be Robert Webb who, ironically, was to become BA's chief in-house lawyer some years later. Sitting with Stelios in Robert Webb's chambers at an early briefing on the case, I smiled at the legal eagle's business card featuring a cartoon alligator and the inscription 'Settle? Where's the fun in that?' I suspected this was one action that wouldn't be settled easily, but we might well have some fun along the way.

On 26th February 1998 easyJet served a writ aimed at stopping the gestating airline in its tracks. It was always going to be a long shot that our legal efforts to prevent Go from taking off would be successful, but we reckoned a high-profile battle would keep us in the headlines – and BA on the back foot. It had the added benefit of distracting Go's senior management and diverting resources away from the herculean task of starting a new airline. At the very least they would have a few sleepless nights worrying about how to deal with tens of thousands of pre-booked passengers if easyJet were to win the case. Undeterred Go pressed on with its launch plans. In early April 1998 they released details of their first routes out of Stansted at return prices starting from £100.

On 13th May 1998, with the new airline in the final stages of preparation for of its launch, Judge Tuckey delivered his

High Court verdict. The application by easyJet for an injunction to stop Go from taking off was refused. There were some crumbs of comfort in the wording of the judgement, the judge having rejected BA's attempt to strike out the writ as baseless. I recall we proclaimed some kind of victory, but with hindsight it didn't really matter. What counted was that nothing now stood in the way of Go becoming a fully-fledged airline and an existential threat to easyJet's survival. The phoney war with what Stelios was now describing as 'BA's low-cost clone' had entered a new phase. The gloves were coming off.

The list of easyJet publicity stunts is certainly a long one. Admittedly not everything we tried was successfully pulled off, but there were quite a few headline-grabbing coups. Arguably, the most effective of all came with the inaugural flight of Go. On the morning that the fledgling airline's tickets went on sale, I called their booking line and bought ten seats on the first flight from Stansted to Rome. The passenger names included my own and that of Stelios, along with several members of the easyJet sales and marketing team. It was naked opportunism, pure and simple. We didn't exactly know what we were going to do, but by booking the seats we gave ourselves two months to plan our tactics. We'd hoped to have the advantage of surprise but Go didn't have an internet booking facility at the time so the booking had to be made by phone. Despite my use of a personal rather than an easyJet credit card, the name 'Stelios Haji-

Ioannou' was instantly recognised by the reservations agent who took the call. Sure enough, when our booking confirmation letters arrived, a polite, personal note had been scribbled on them by Barbara Cassani, wishing us a pleasant flight. I very much doubt that she meant it. Go's chief executive had no idea of what was headed her way.

The big day came; Friday 22nd May 1998. It was a beautiful sunny morning, in marked contrast to the overcast skies that had accompanied easyJet's inaugural flight three years earlier. An anonymous white transit van left Luton airport in the early hours with a big surprise for British Airways on-board. Traffic on the roads was light and our small group arrived at the Stansted Hilton just before 7 a.m. We changed into specially commissioned bright-orange boiler suits. The outfits were emblazoned on the front with the easyJet logo, each had a single letter printed in white on the reverse. Stelios was the 'G' and I was the 'e'. When we stood in line, the letters spelled 'Go, easyJet'. The orange team was in high spirits as we posed for photographs outside the hotel.

In good time for check-in, we showed up at the airport in our colourful garb. The look on the faces of Go's PR team had to be seen to be believed. In desperation, someone called the airport police, suggesting there had been a breach of the peace. Within a matter of minutes a couple of armed officers arrived on the scene. They found the whole situation highly amusing and concluded we were doing nothing wrong. The television cameras turned away from Go's press spokesman and towards the orange interlopers. On the face of it Barbara Cassani was taking the upstaging with good grace. She attempted to present easyJet's chairman with his own outsized boarding pass, but inwardly I suspected she was seething. If Stelios was feeling any guilt, he certainly wasn't showing it. I can still recall the huge smile on his face as he walked up and down the aisle of the Rome-bound plane, dispensing free easyJet flight vouchers to eager Go passengers. The journalists whom Go had invited to travel on its inaugural flight flocked to the back of the plane to interview the owner of their biggest rival. It was quite a coup and the marketing team celebrated with an ice cream on the Spanish Steps in the centre of Rome.

I travelled back from the Italian capital on a flight operated by yet another low-cost operator, the bizarrely named *Debonair*. Under the leadership of veteran airline executive, Franco Mancassola, they had opted for the middle ground between low-cost and full-service that was to prove disastrous for a number of other start-up airlines, including KLM's *Buzz*. *Debonair* had launched just nine months after easyJet, initially operating two leased aircraft serving three routes; from Luton to Munich, Dusseldorf and Barcelona. Further cities including Madrid, Newcastle, Copenhagen and Rome had followed soon after. Ostensibly *Debonair* was targeting the business traveller offering 'low-cost with a few frills', a concept I likened to being 'half-pregnant' and equally unviable. The flaws in their business model were compounded by a decision to operate the BAe 146-200 aircraft rather than the larger and more cost-effective 737s chosen by easyJet, Ryanair and Southwest. It was the airline equivalent of bringing a knife to a gunfight, with a similar probability of outcomes.

The financial success of the low-cost model in North America and the early promise shown by easyJet had drawn the eye of potential investors. With astute timing, *Debonair* successfully raised £25m in a share issue in the summer of 1997. I wasn't convinced; from that point on it was simply a question of how long the money would last.

An early and, as it turned out, rather prescient poster advertisement, showed their finance director at Franco's feet, in tears at the low fares it was offering. The airline's results for 1997 revealed a loss of £15m on a turnover of not much more, it was clearly unsustainable. In the autumn of 1999 with financial pressure intensifying, *Debonair* put out feelers to easyJet. I went with Stelios to visit Franco in his Luton offices. He was charming, cracked some good jokes and served proper Italian coffee – but it was clear his airline was a busted flush. They had absolutely nothing to offer us. As we walked out through their car park, Stelios joked to me that their only asset of any value was Franco's Alfa Romeo. On 2nd October 1999 the vet was called to put the ailing carrier out of its misery and *Debonair* went into administration. The airline's 14-strong fleet was immediately grounded and 750 of its passengers were left stranded overseas. We issued a press release pinning the blame on British Airways. Stelios said BA had 'blood on its hands'.

Chapter Nineteen

Stop Go

Debonair was a sideshow; our minds were focussed on the more serious long-term challenge posed by Go. As predicted, they had chosen to base themselves at Stansted. The three launch routes (Milan, Rome and Copenhagen) had avoided head-to-head competition with easyJet. It was a deliberately low-key start but within three months they upped the ante. On 11 August 1998, Go announced a new service, flying three times daily to Edinburgh at similar times and at similar fares to those offered by easyJet. Stelios was not happy, to put it mildly – on hearing the news he reacted immediately, dictating a full-page newspaper advertisement from the back of a London taxi. The ad was headlined 'Mother of all fare wars'.

In October 1998 the war he had declared 'went nuclear' when Go introduced a £15 one-way fare between Stansted and Edinburgh, undercutting easyJet's lowest price of £29. With the original legal action in the UK courts still rumbling along in the background, an additional complaint was lodged with the

European Competition Authorities alleging predatory pricing and cross-subsidisation.

A ding-dong advertising and PR battle between the two carriers soon developed. Instead of simply rolling with the punches, Go was now fighting back, and giving easyJet a taste of its own medicine. When a dusting of snow closed Luton airport, they took out ads saying 'Would you rather fly with the airline most likely to get you there or the airline with a generous refund policy because they don't?' David Magliano, Go's sales and marketing director, celebrated its triumph in the 'best low-cost carrier' airline category at a prestigious awards ceremony by taking a long-term poster site close to easyJet's headquarters.

Weathering the storm of provocative advertising and constant sniping in the media from its orange rival, Go continued to expand. A new hub was opened in Bristol and the Stansted operation was scaled up, offering new services to a host of summer sun destinations. The brand enjoyed high levels of customer advocacy and was now carving out its own space independently of British Airways. Commentators began referring to them as 'the Waitrose of the airline business.'

The battle moved closer to easyLand when Go poached a number of key staff, including aircraft operations chief, Andy Holmes, and Mike Coltman, easyJet's contracts manager. There was more than a hint of irony as Mike had been among the orange clad hijackers of our rival's first flight. I viewed this as a smart move on Go's part. I'd got to know him during our memorable visit to observe Southwest Airlines operations in New Orleans. He was a clever guy, personable and charismatic with a wicked sense of humour. More than anyone, Mike understood the importance of company culture and the role it had played in the Southwest success story.

With the new millennium approaching, I thought hard about my personal future. The airline was now profitable and, despite the competition, was more than holding its own. I thought, wrongly as it transpired, this might be the high-water mark for easyJet. The wider business world was in turmoil, traditional thinking turned upside-down by the internet revolution. Fortunes were being made overnight by the brave and the bold. All the action was taking place in the virtual arena. Increasingly the aviation industry looked like a bit of a backwater.

Stelios took me to one side and told me the time had come to activate his long-standing plans to establish new ventures under the 'easy' brand. As marketing director of the 'easyGroup', I would be its first employee, working with him to develop and launch these new ideas. The first of these would be a string of giant internet cafés throughout Europe and, eventually, the world (well, it seemed a good idea at the time!). In keeping with the trend for internet related companies to have off-beat names like *Yahoo* and *Alta Vista* we called it *easyEverything*.

Stelios's plan was to super-size the internet café, creating 4-600 seater behemoths with floor space of between 15,000 and 20,000 square feet. The outlets were to operate 24 hours a day and income would be derived from the sale of advertising, refreshments as well as internet time. Another concept on the drawing board was *easyRentacar*, a pan-European internet-based car rental start-up, featuring a single vehicle type, the Mercedes A-class and offering prices well below industry norms. I would be made a director both of the easyGroup and the new start-ups as well as being given a chance to invest (on a small scale) alongside him.

It was not an easy decision; leaving easyJet would mean stepping away from the battle with British Airways just when it was getting interesting. Yet it was clear that, although the airline was continuing to grow fast, it was maturing and entering a new phase. There was another factor at play. I'd started to develop differences of opinion with Ray Webster, the managing director (and later chief executive) whom Stelios had brought in from *Air New Zealand.*

Ray, a trained engineer with many years of airline experience, had an analytical approach that contrasted markedly with my strong reliance on intuition. He was to play the key role in guiding easyJet through its successful flotation and deserves significant credit for the airline's success. As I wavered, Stelios counselled that I was better at starting things up and growing them in the early stages and that now was the time to move on. It was hard advice to swallow, but I shook his hand and accepted the offer. At an emotional leaving party to celebrate the move to easyGroup, I was presented with the bright-orange boiler suit I'd worn on our famous Go raid a few months earlier.

While I was dealing with the challenges of starting new easy-branded businesses in the white heat of the internet boom years, Go continued to build its network, slowly inching towards profitability. With its budget offspring now firmly established, tensions began to develop within British Airways over the future of a potential problem child. Go's success had started to raise questions about competition with its larger parent on European routes. On 2nd November 1999 traffic figures published by the British Airports Authority showed that British Airways was losing market share to the low-cost airlines. Their passenger numbers had dropped by 4.9% compared with an increase of 5% for the market as a whole. By now, Bob Ayling – who'd got BA into the low-cost game in the first place – was on his way out. His replacement as Chief Executive was to be an Australian, Rod Eddington, a man on a mission to strengthen the flag carrier's financial position. He immediately embarked on a programme of cost-cutting and rationalisation. Serious belt tightening was involved.

Speculation intensified that BA's low-cost airline was in play. In August 2000, an article in *The Sunday Times* reported that Go had been valued at £200 million and that easyJet were considering a bid. In reality, secret talks between British Airways and Stelios had taken place some weeks earlier but had foundered because BA wanted cash rather than untraded shares in easyJet, at that point still an unlisted company. The issue looked to have been settled early in 2001 when, following an auction, BA announced that it was to sell Go to a management-buyout team working in partnership with private-equity group, 3i. The move made a lot of sense: Cassani and team were leading the airline through a phase of sustained growth while muttering inside BA that Go was cannibalising its parent's European business had intensified. Most commentators assumed that the new owners would recoup their investment by floating the airline at some point down the line. I'd assumed that any exit would be at least three years off.

Then in May 2002 came the bombshell. In a truly audacious move, easyJet announced it was to take-over arch rival, Go, in a transaction valued at £374 million. The industry's tectonic plates had shifted. The combined entity would have fifty-four aircraft and passenger numbers that topped twelve million. The BBC's business correspondent Jeff Randall closed a news item with the words 'Now, it seems, the future is orange'. Even Ryanair chief executive Michael O'Leary seemed impressed, saying, 'I will be taking lessons in humility now that we are – for the time being – Europe's second-largest low-fare airline'. Along with the aircraft deal, easyJet inherited established bases at Bristol, East Midlands and Stansted. The distinctive brand that David Magliano and the rest of the Go marketing team had worked so hard to build was deemed surplus to requirements.

There was to be no change at the helm. Ray Webster remained as chief executive of the enlarged airline and Barbara Cassani exited stage left, several million pounds to the good. The deal catapulted easyJet into the Premier League of European airlines and consolidated Stelios's reputation as a dealmaker and a real player in global aviation. After years of fighting toe to toe with British Airways, he'd landed a knockout punch. The 800-pound gorilla had hit the canvas and his victory over them was complete.

Chapter Twenty

Going Dutch

Although it began life as a domestic operator, shuttling up and down to Scotland, easyJet had been conceived from the start, as a pan-European airline. The size of the European market as a whole was comparable to the United States, where the low-cost model had already proven its long-term viability. The scale of the financial opportunity may have been similar, but an airline expanding into Europe faced a number of additional challenges. These included language, culture and local labour laws. Furthermore in comparison with the UK, continental Europe had lower levels of credit card ownership and there were powerful vested interests at national level. We couldn't afford to spend millions adapting our model to meet the needs of individual markets. In any case, complexity carries with it significant long-term costs. If easyJet was to work as a truly European airline, it would need as standardised and simple an approach as possible. In the words of Stelios, we needed to develop a 'cookie cutter'.

A key advantage of the 'David versus Goliath' formula – apart from its inherent simplicity – is that it was applicable to virtually all the markets we were intending to enter. Every European country had an incumbent national airline and, to a greater or lesser degree, each had grown fat and lazy over the years under the protective umbrella of state ownership and a regulated market. Hardly surprising, therefore, that we employed the same tried and tested formula when we made our first foray into Europe with the launch of our Luton to Amsterdam service in April 1996.

The choice of route was entirely logical, though strangely it hadn't featured in the original easyJet business plan. At that time, Holland was Europe's second most deregulated air-transport market and its capital, Amsterdam, was among the UK's leading short-break destinations. The city was also the home turf of Dutch national carrier, KLM, an industry heavyweight that could be counted firmly in the 800-pound gorilla category. With a history stretching back to 1919, KLM was the oldest commercial airline in the world and a source of considerable pride for many Dutch nationals. The airline's longevity derived from a long-standing domination of its small domestic market, a respected brand and a pre-eminent position at Amsterdam's Schiphol airport, a key international hub.

As deregulation gathered pace, the more progressive elements at KLM could see the way the wind was blowing.

Under the leadership of chief executive, Pieter Bouw, the airline had begun the painful process of restructuring to meet the challenges of liberalisation. The path they were following was similar to that favoured by British Airways. Departments had been closed or merged, headcount reduced, vanity routes shut down and a customer service ethos established. But if they thought this would be sufficient to deter the new breed of low-cost carriers from entering the Dutch market they were mistaken.

Stakes for the airline poker game had gone up considerably, necessitating substantial further investment. Noise restrictions meant Schipol airport was off-limits to the existing leased aircraft. Instead the route would be operated by easyJet's newly acquired Boeing 737-300. The addition to the orange fleet was a larger, quieter and more fuel efficient aircraft equipped with 148 seats compared to the 130 passenger capacity of the older 737-200s. Filling three return flights daily at 80% capacity required 700 bums on seats, each day, every day. Furthermore, Schipol's high airport charges meant the base fare was set at £39 rather than the £29 for which easyJet had become known. It was a formidable challenge for the marketing team to get its teeth into.

Our growing base of satisfied customers coupled with strong brand awareness in Luton and the surrounding counties, gave me confidence we could generate sales at the UK end of the route. We launched our service with a headline-grabbing offer. Amsterdam priced at 39p for all seats on the first day, exclusively promoted through the *Daily Mirror*. But, for the route to be profitable, we'd also need to generate sales from the Dutch market where the brand was completely unknown. To meet this challenge I'd taken on Ivar Gribnau, a young, ambitious graduate from the University of Leiden. He was looking to break into the airline business and wouldn't take no for an answer. The job of marketing manager for the Netherlands was never advertised. Ivar simply badgered me for days on end with telephone calls from Holland offering his services. In the end, worn down by his persistence, I agreed to an interview just to get the guy off my back. It proved to be a smart move on my part. Not only was Ivar a great find, we'd also stumbled on a formula that would serve us well. For each new market we appointed someone to the role of national marketing manager, giving them responsibility for getting 'bums on seats' in their part of the world.

In advance of the first flight, we placed advertisements highlighting KLM's high fares in the major newspapers. Over the years the Dutch airline's marketing had consistently featured images of swans, perhaps in the belief that people would come to associate the elegant and graceful birds with a lumbering airline. Our opening shot was a newspaper ad which showed a dazed looking, seemingly punch-drunk, swan and the tag-line '*het jachtseizoen is geopend*' literally translated as 'The hunting season has started'. No other airline had previously dared to attack KLM in such a direct fashion and we immediately drew the attention of the Dutch media.

There was more to come. A high-intensity poster campaign painted the tourist areas of Amsterdam orange. We managed to secure the key sites in and around the city, having engaged the services of Jaap Boender, a media specialist who knew the Dutch market inside out. Just as BA had done before it, KLM steadfastly ignored our provocation and maintained a stony silence. It was time to poke them with a sharp stick. Stelios came up with a good idea: in advance of our launch, we'd printed coupons in our in-flight magazine, inviting passengers to complain about the ridiculously high price of flights to Amsterdam. This had solicited a massive response which we bagged up in four large sacks before setting off to hand deliver them to the KLM chairman at the airline's headquarters located close to Schiphol airport. Camera crews were following our every move. Needless to say, we were turned away at the security gatehouse (although a KLM representative did at least have the good grace to come down and collect our gift for their chairman). A specially staged press conference was well attended by the media (though ignored by KLM). That evening, easyJet made prime-time news on all the major TV channels.

Provoked by the positive coverage we were receiving, the Dutch carrier could contain itself no longer. KLM released a press statement in which they rubbished the no-frills concept and explained why it wasn't going to work in their home market. A spokesman was actually quoted as saying Dutch people didn't like low fares. It was manna from heaven. Within minutes of our press conference going on air, the phone calls started coming through. The Dutch, it seemed, liked low fares after all.

On 24th April 1996, easyJet's first international flight landed at Amsterdam's Schiphol Airport; needless to say it was full. As Stelios stepped off the aircraft, a welcoming committee presented him with a bunch of orange tulips. He posed for photographs on the aircraft steps, before heading off to a press conference and the first of many interviews. There was a real buzz in the air. It felt more like a homecoming than his airline's first foray onto foreign soil.

Despite the positive start, I was acutely aware this was a marathon not a sprint and remained alert to the possibility if not the likelihood of underhand tactics. There was a whiff of foul play in the air at Schiphol Airport where easyJet was assigned check-in desks alongside Israeli airline *El Al* in a segregated area adjacent to the main departure hall. Customers were undeterred; price, it seemed, was conquering all and the mild inconvenience failed to deter a growing clientele from choosing easyJet.

For all their public denials, KLM were undoubtedly worried by the arrival of low-cost competition on their doorstep. In the years leading up to 1996 they had built up a 45 per cent stake in the British regional carrier *Air UK*. Lacking the strong brand and distribution network of BA, the part-owned airline had been taking a pasting at the hands of easyJet on the Anglo-Scottish routes. I sensed opinion within KLM was polarising, between a group who wanted to continue to ignore what was happening and those who had seen what happened to *Air UK* and advocated a more proactive stance. If such a debate was going on, the second group appeared to have won the argument. Having lost the opening round, KLM came out fighting when the bell sounded. Within a matter of weeks of easyJet's launch in the Dutch market, they began introducing price reductions on flights between London and Amsterdam. Their lowest fare of 190 Dutch guilders undercut easyJet and was headlined in advertisements as being 'an easy choice'. KLM's actions triggered an allegation that they were engaged in predatory pricing. There was a distinct feeling of déjà vu about what followed.

Stelios went to the European Commission, bolstered by the uncovering of an internal memo that allegedly called for 'a determined campaign to stop the growth and development of easyJet'. The Competition Commission has sharp teeth, with the ability to impose fines of up to ten per cent of turnover for offenders. The Commission's action likely caused other flag carriers throughout Europe to sit up and take notice. Though the complaint ended up going nowhere, the ongoing battle was widely discussed in the media. On radio phone-ins, TV chat shows and newspaper columns, everyone was talking about easyJet. You wouldn't have thought that the airline flew just a single route between Luton and Amsterdam. Our profile among the Dutch public was out of all proportion to our size.

Once again we benefitted from being in the right place at the right time, as the Euro '96 football tournament got underway in England. Orange was the colour of the Dutch team and easyJet was adopted as the unofficial airline of the nation by thousands of their enthusiastic supporters flying into Luton. The fans were vocal and high spirited but a credit to their country. They queued to have their photo taken as they boarded the orange liveried planes or with their arm around a member of the easyJet cabin crew. Even the team's 4-1 thrashing at the hands of England failed to dampen their enthusiasm. The main Dutch TV station filmed an outside broadcast using the orange offices at easyLand as a backdrop. I took it as a sign that we had successfully ridden our luck. In a few short months and at relatively low cost we had gone from being an unknown company to a recognised brand in the Dutch market.

As easyJet built on its early success and brand recognition, KLM's bold statement that the Dutch people didn't want low fares came to haunt them. More capacity was added to the Luton route and services from Amsterdam to Liverpool and Nice were launched. For more than three years a shell-shocked KLM watched in disbelief and denial as the orange upstart took everything they could throw at it. Despite their actions the brand flourished on their doorstep. On 16th October 1999, in a belated acknowledgement that the low-cost model had something to offer after all, KLM announced the creation of *Buzz*, its own low-cost carrier based at Stansted airport. The airline was a purple and yellow liveried monstrosity as useless and pointless as the children's TV character, *Barney the Dinosaur* from which it appeared to have derived its colour scheme.

Buzz was doomed from the start: not only was the business model hopelessly compromised, but the airline chose to operate with a mixed fleet, including the infamous British Aerospace 146, an aircraft totally unsuited to a low-cost operation. For a few short years, the airline struggled to establish itself in a low-cost market that was now starting to look crowded. The airline's average load factors regularly dipped below 50 per cent and losses mounted. As a wounded *Buzz* bled cash, KLM started looking for a way out, exploring options for a sale or merger. The airline's demise was like falling off a cliff in slow motion, the eventual outcome was predictable but it was painful to watch. In January 2003 *Buzz* was taken over, swallowed up and spat out by Ryanair. Few mourned its passing.

Chapter Twenty One

Expansion into Europe

Throughout 1996 and into 1997, easyJet's expansion to the continent gathered momentum. The versatility of the giant-killer marketing formula was demonstrated to great effect. A few months after Amsterdam, Nice became the next stop on our grand European tour. The city's airport was the gateway to the French Riviera, memorably described by writer Somerset Maugham as being 'a sunny place for shady people'. The new service brought us into direct competition with Air France for the first time, though our key opponent was, once again, British Airways. The UK's national carrier dominated the route with high-frequency services to Nice from several airports. You only had to watch the passengers checking in for their flight to appreciate there was a substantial well-heeled clientele. The route was a well-established money spinner for BA, but prices had been too high for too long. Lower fares would stimulate the market and generate sufficient demand to fill easyJet's planes. British people with second homes in the region were a key target market, and word of mouth was very strong among this group. We were receiving several calls a week from property owners, pleading for us to start flights to the Riviera. As launch efforts started to gear up, support came from an unexpected quarter. I had expected easyJet to be treated with Gallic indifference by the French airport authorities but instead of shrugging their shoulders they seemed to welcome the arrival of competition to British Airways. The marketing director of Nice Airport, Clive Raymond, was a forward thinker and backed easyJet to succeed. Unlike most of his contemporaries, he could see how both the airport and the wider regional economy might benefit from the arrival of a low-cost carrier.

On 05th June 1996 we launched the new route with a bang, flying sixty prize winners from three UK regional radio stations to Nice for a party at local nightspot, Wayne's Bar. Stelios was in celebratory mood: he would no longer have to fly to his home in Monaco on a competitor airline. For the first time, I spotted him on the dance floor, strutting his stuff to the sound of the classic Oasis track 'Don't Look Back in Anger'. It was far from elegant but nobody cared; the champagne was flowing and the party was in full swing.

The prize winners had been accompanied to Nice by presenters from the commercial radio stations involved. The event proved a sound investment – we got great coverage from the launch party, not to mention plenty of on-air messages for our new service. For once, we didn't really need it. We didn't even need to put a provocative poster above the British Airways sales desk at Nice airport, but we did it anyway – and it felt pretty good! Fares were higher than for the domestic routes, with prices between £49 and £99 each way. For the following year's Monaco Grand Prix weekend we introduced a fare of £199. Practically all the seats on the most popular flights carrying F1 fans to and from the race were at the highest fare. I worried we might have overdone it, but we sold out within a couple of days. British Airways were accustomed to pushing their prices as high as £700 at that time of year. We could have sold out our flights many times over. In the space of twelve months easyJet had taken a 25 per cent market share of passenger traffic between London and Nice. For the first time since our launch we were inflicting real financial pain on British Airways. If we hadn't previously had the attention of Europe's aviation giants, we certainly had it now.

There was no time for self-congratulation, the next route awaited. A pattern had been established and we moved speedily onto Spain and the Catalan capital, Barcelona. The city was a popular short-break destination with UK travellers, underserved and with plenty of potential to grow. Our newly appointed marketing manager, Christina Bernabe, knew exactly what to do. We adopted the same approach that had served us so well on previous occasions, achieving a similar result. The Spanish and

Catalan media clamoured for interviews with Stelios and he duly obliged. Perhaps deterred by coverage of previous legal actions, the national carrier, *Iberia*, didn't even attempt to drop its fares. On 14th June 1996 an orange aircraft packed full of British holiday makers touched down at Barcelona airport. The route proved an instant hit, the market for short breaks to Barcelona mushroomed almost overnight. Plans for new services to the Spanish cities of Malaga and Madrid were brought forward.

I'd run out of fingers on which to count the number of routes easyJet was now flying. Our UK advertising was becoming more cost-effective since we were now able to list multiple destinations in our press ads. Once again, we reprinted our expanding timetable, this time with a picture showing our growing European route network on the reverse.

Computer analysis of our passenger's postcodes showed that, with the launch of international services, easyJet's catchment area had widened: we were now attracting customers from across the country. A significant proportion of them were travelling down to Luton from the north of England. In the spring of 1997, negotiations began with the owners of Liverpool airport with a view to making it easyJet's second UK base. Speke airport (since renamed Liverpool John Lennon Airport) had been in the shadow of its larger rival, Manchester, for many years. Like Luton two years earlier, Liverpool airport was underused. Owners, the Peel Group, were ambitious, and there was a deal to be done. On a visit up to Liverpool to assess opportunities for branding our airport presence, I was struck by the similarities with Luton two years earlier. We moved quickly: by November 1997, easyJet was operating flights to both Amsterdam and Nice from its new base.

The centres of Manchester and Liverpool turned a familiar shade of orange as easyJet switched on the advertising tap. Adding cities to the growing network was becoming a bit formulaic. But as the airline's reputation grew and the brand gathered strength we found ourselves having to spend a lower proportion of revenues on promoting new routes. We were also starting to tone down the messaging; self-censoring the brainstormed slogan 'Fly with easyJet to Amsterdam and the only thing that's wasted is you'.

Opening a second UK base gave easyJet some important strategic leverage with Luton airport, the ownership of which was rumoured to be on the verge of changing hands. With easyJet projecting rapid growth and other low-cost airlines knocking on Luton's door, a new owner might be tempted to impose higher airport charges. In this eventuality, having the option of putting additional capacity into Liverpool rather than Luton would be a useful bargaining chip – and a potential insurance policy.

Less than two years had passed since our first flight, but we had proved the low-cost model worked in Europe and that easyJet was financially viable. The time had come for Stelios to spend real money. By September 1997, he felt sufficiently confident to place an order for twelve new Boeing 737-300 aircraft. List price would have been in excess of $500m. The extent to which Stelios finally managed to bargain them down was a carefully guarded secret. With the deal agreed, Boeing bosses rashly offered to take the easyJet senior management team to the restaurant of our choice for a celebratory dinner. Stelios had no hesitation in nominating the world famous *Hotel de Paris* restaurant in Monaco, renowned for its mouth-watering food and eye-watering prices. It would mean putting on a tie for the evening – only the second time I'd had to wear one since joining easyJet – but the meal was worth it, and I like to think we put a small dent in Boeing's annual profits that evening!

Stelios's Greek Cypriot heritage meant that our launch of services between London and Athens in the summer of 1998 was always going to be a high-profile battle. However, in one respect we were faced with an unusual and unprecedented dilemma. Olympic Airlines, the Greek flag carrier, was in a truly parlous financial state and there was no PR mileage to be had in picking on such an obviously weak competitor. Instead, our attention turned back to an old enemy in the shape of the Greek travel agency community. We ran a series of impolite, mocking ads encouraging the travelling public to cut out the middleman. Yannis Capodistrias, our marketing manager on the ground in Athens, reported that things were heating up nicely. The federation of Greek travel agents reacted angrily accusing easyJet of 'commercial hooliganism'. Legal action then ensued. The federation obtained a court injunction preventing us from running the ads in the Greek press. Among other things they complained bitterly of the threat easyJet posed to their livelihoods. We responded by painting the offending expression in two-meter-high lettering on the side of one of our aircraft before flying it down to Athens.

The confrontation with the travel agents culminated in a court appearance in Athens by Stelios himself. Prior to the court hearing, easyJet's chairman had announced that he would be offering vouchers for free flights to London to anyone who turned out to support him at the trial. On emerging from the courtroom, Stelios was greeted by a horde of people chanting his name, all anxious to get their hands on the free flight vouchers. Among them, a number of travel agents were spotted. A chaotic scene developed, with the crowd scrambling for the vouchers as easyJet's call-centre manager, John MacLeod, doubling as Stelios's unofficial minder, fought to extract his boss from the melee. Happily, the only lasting injuries were those to the pride of the Greek travel-agency community. Indeed, the whole incident has become part of easyJet folklore.

In the spring of 1998, easyJet turned its attention to the lucrative Swiss market. Switzerland was not a member of the European Union and was not, therefore, bound by the European Open Skies agreements that had done so much to open up free market competition between national airlines accustomed to cosy duopolies. Both conventional and low-cost carriers looked on the Zurich and Geneva routes with greedy eyes as the seasonality of skiing traffic complimented the summer sun destinations that generated so much of their revenue. The frequency of flights to places such as Malaga, Faro and Alicante could be cut back for the winter, with the aircraft redeployed to pick up the skiing market.

But, without the support of the regulators in Brussels, there was only one way to build a sizeable operation between the UK and Switzerland – and that was through the acquisition of an existing Swiss carrier. Stelios got to hear that a Swiss part-charter, part-scheduled operator called *TEA Basle* was running into difficulties. On 26th March 1998 it was reported in the *Financial Times* that he had snapped up a share in the carrier for a budget price of 3 million Swiss francs. Following completion of the deal, the airline's base was moved from Basle to Geneva and easyJet Switzerland was born. With frequent, low-cost flights from London to (first) Geneva and (later) Zurich, easyJet rapidly took market share from British Airways and *Swissair* who could scarcely believe what was happening to them. In

March 1998 easyJet announced that it was intending to operate flights out of Switzerland to other European destinations. At this point the fight started to turn dirty. Behind the scenes *Swissair* was working desperately to put obstacles in easyJet's way. In a press conference at the Forum Park hotel in Geneva, Stelios accused them of lobbying the Swiss government to block easyJet's flights from Geneva to Barcelona that were due to start operating at the end of the month.

On 14th July 1999 the Swiss transport minister ruled that easyJet could not compete on the Geneva-Barcelona route because Swissair had a protected monopoly. A furious Stelios described Swissair as 'the evil empire' and declared Chairman Philip Buggier to be Darth Vader. A fortnight later easyJet Switzerland's first flight to Barcelona took off. A message applied by decal to the side of the aircraft declared 'Monopole de Swissair: Non'. In compliance with the court's ruling, all passengers had been refunded. Stelios made an announcement on board the inaugural flight explaining his battle against *Swissair* and its allies. He then passed a hat (some contend it was actually a bucket) around and collected 2,700 Swiss francs in voluntary contributions from passengers. It was a nice touch which grabbed the headlines but you can't run an airline funded through charitable donations. What easyJet needed was a way of highlighting the intrinsic unfairness of the protectionist ruling and getting the wider Swiss public on its side. That's where the tents came in …

Above the easyLand reception there used to hang a small, nondescript two-man tent. Visitors to the airline's headquarters were often puzzled to see it hanging there. Those that asked were surprised to learn that this was an unlikely trophy of a famous victory over *Swissair*. The carrier's attempts to block easyJet's operations between Geneva and Barcelona were based on an arcane ruling that its low-cost flights must come with accommodation provided. To adhere to the legal technicalities, easyJet erected three orange tents on the side of a hill, one hundred and fifty kilometres north of Barcelona. The tents cost the princely sum of £29.99 each from *Argos*. Only a handful of hardy souls ever stayed in them.

The move was widely reported in the Swiss media, not only exposing the device which, easyJet believed, was being employed to keep them out of the market, but also turning the national carrier into a laughing stock. An orange tent was put on display at Geneva airport. Calls and internet enquiries from customers based in Switzerland rose sharply. Eventually, the Swiss authorities – undoubtedly embarrassed – dropped their objections. Routes from Geneva to a range of destinations, including Nice, Amsterdam, Belfast and Madrid, were launched soon afterwards. Passenger volumes on the new routes were significantly higher than anticipated. The easyJet brand had well and truly been established in the Swiss market.

A bruised and battered *Swissair* staggered on for a couple more years, tottering like a mortally wounded giant on the financial precipice. Following the September 11 attacks, their position worsened significantly. In October 2001 the airline that had fought Canute-like to stem the low-cost tide was grounded. They were kept on financial life support by the Swiss Federal government for a few more months before finally ceasing operations. The once-proud national symbol had become one more name on a lengthening casualty list in a brutally unforgiving industry. The industry-wide downturn following the twin towers attacks was undoubtedly the final nail in the coffin. However, the romantic in me likes to think that a few flimsy tents also played a part in their downfall. It's just a shame that, in recording for posterity the quasi-Shakespearean tragedy of *Swissair's* demise, the newspaper editors missed an opportunity to use the headline derived from the Bard's work *Richard III*: 'Now is the winter of our discount tent'.

As the new millennium dawned, easyJet's foothold on the continent was firmly established, despite the best efforts of the legacy carriers they would not be easily dislodged. Turnover had grown from nothing to £263 million in the space of just five years. More significantly the airline was now profitable to the tune of some £22m. On 15 November 2000 an oversubscribed share offering saw easyJet floated on the London Stock Exchange. By the close of trading the company was valued at £777 million.

With a number of European aviation heavyweights on their backs and others sporting black eyes and bloody noses, this chapter of the easyJet story draws to a close. The initial forays into Europe had shone light into some of the darkest corners of state protectionism. What amazed me, perhaps more than anything, was how flag carriers faced with the entry of a low-cost airline into their markets had repeated the same basic mistakes.

The time for denial was over. Far from covertly resisting or grudgingly accepting easyJet's arrival, European airports were now welcoming the airline with open arms. Liz Savage, easyJet's talented business development manager was inundated with emails and telephone calls from airports across the continent. Stelios was hailed by the business community as an inspirational and far-sighted leader. Those legacy carriers who had not already started, set about major strategic re-evaluations of their long-term futures in a new European aviation market where low-cost travel took centre stage. Somewhere in west London, an un-named British Airways spokesman was choking on his peanuts.

Chapter Twenty Two

Don't look back in anger

It's true. As you get older time passes more quickly. Anniversaries of all kinds come and go seemingly in the blink of an eye. To think it's over four years since I was sat freezing my butt off in an aircraft hangar at Luton celebrating the 20th anniversary of easyJet's first flight in 1995. What a surreal occasion that was. A bizarrely hubristic event featuring flag-waving employees from bases across the continent parading with fixed smiles in front of an audience of the world's media and 400 VIP guests. More *Eurovision*-style extravaganza than the birthday party of a low-cost airline.

The 2020 celebration will mark easyJet's quarter century. Yes, it really is that long since flight EZY 11 lifted off the Luton airport tarmac en-route to Glasgow. Twenty-five years in which generation easyJet has grown up and come of age. The impact on European aviation has been unimaginable. Hundreds of millions of people across the continent today take low-cost air travel for granted. The notion that tickets to travel were once bought from a high street shop and that hot meals were served free of charge to all on board seem equally implausible.

New carriers have come and gone. A small number have put down roots and become established in the arid soil of European aviation. But the two airlines who were there at the start now dominate the continent, testimony perhaps to the concept of first-mover advantage.

Ryanair's claim to be top dog is hard to dispute. The carrier now forms part of a larger group comprising Ryanair itself and three smaller sister companies. Together they now fly more international passengers than any other airline in the world. Their business model remains fundamentally unchanged: full flights at low prices to places you've never heard of, tightly managed costs and an industry leading level of ancillary sales. In July 2019 the *Telegraph* reported that the amount of revenue collected by Ryanair for optional extras such as baggage charges and seat selection fees had risen to $2.8 billion – a figure that exceeded the GDPs of 30 different countries.

Anyone who feared Michael O'Leary's sense of humour might have diminished with the passage of time can rest easy. The once-ridiculed *Buzz* brand has been dug up from the unhallowed ground where it has lain buried the past seventeen years and now adorns the aircraft of Ryanair's Polish low-cost subsidiary. O'Leary takes more of a back seat these days, having relinquished day-to-day control of his much maligned airline to a trusted lieutenant. I freely admit to having underestimated him. Then again, most people did.

As for Mr easyJet himself … knighted in 2006 for services to entrepreneurship, Sir Stelios Haji-Ioannou is no longer chairman or even a director of the airline he founded, yet remains its largest and most vocal shareholder. Like an ardent football fan shouting advice to his team from the stands and keeping management permanently on their toes. There appears to be no prospect of imminent retirement. Today easyJet's founder spends a significant proportion of his time running the eponymous Stelios Philanthropic Foundation, which supports charitable activities in the UK, Greece, Cyprus and Monaco.

Although now displaced by Gatwick as easyJet's largest base, Luton remains the airline's spiritual home. A cosmopolitan, post-industrial town grappling with a host of social challenges, but outward looking and hopeful for the future, buoyed by investment and jobs created through the airport's thriving economic eco-system. The airport itself has finally emerged from a long-running, passenger punishing redevelopment and continues to cover itself in glory. In 2018, the Consumer Association's *Which* magazine awarded Luton the title of UK's worst airport for a record-breaking third year in succession.

The architectural eyesore we affectionately nicknamed 'easyLand' is no more. By chance I was passing through Luton airport the day the developer's bulldozers reduced it to a smoking pile of rubble and corrugated sheeting. In death, as in life, the building was as ugly as sin. But, over time, a bit like the Elephant Man, we had come to love it. Less than two hundred metres away stands its replacement. Bearing the Orwellian sounding name 'Hangar 89', this orange monolith assails the eyes of arriving passengers with a silent tangerine scream as they emerge, blinking, from the Luton terminal. Looking for all the world like the lair of a latter day Bond villain, the vast edifice hums with activity. Orange-clad personnel scurry to and fro, engaged in all manner of tasks required to keep a fleet of over 300 aircraft in the air. Within its walls the once-vibrant easyJet call centre has long since fallen silent, a casualty of the all-conquering internet.

The planes too are different; Boeing has been replaced by Airbus as easyJet's manufacturer of choice and a new livery adorns the fleet. Am I alone in thinking the redesigned aircraft now resembles a wrapped chocolate you might pluck from a box of *Celebrations*? Inside the cabin; the orange has been toned down, while the casual crew uniforms have become progressively slicker, smarter and more corporate.

The airline's marketers (the male ones, at least), now more likely to be sporting hipster-style beards than ponytails, go about their creative work. Efforts of the past look crude and clunky in comparison. They paint with a steadier hand, a finer brush and a more sophisticated palette. Stylish branding advertisements and television spots vie for international awards. A prominent display cabinet in reception glitters with trophies, awards and accolades. The aggressive advertising that was a hallmark of the carrier's rapid growth phase has been ditched overboard. David versus Goliath no longer holds water when you fly twice as many passengers as your closest UK-based rival.

The 'Auld Enemy' is still there, of course, British Airways now melded with *Iberia* to form the *International Airlines Group*. The airline lurks Gollum-like in the shadows of European aviation, muttering of past glories and the 'precious' hold it once exerted over the UK's business travellers. Having ridden out the low-cost revolution it has emerged leaner, meaner and doubtless longing to kick some orange butt.

From the customer's perspective, the passing years have seen new routes, more choice along with some distinctly unwelcome developments. The days when the price you were quoted was the price you paid are long gone. Today, the final cost is inflated by government taxes, luggage charges and credit card fees. The airline's website resembles a vast online bazaar whose persistent electronic merchants whisper siren-like in your ear as they wedge their virtual foot in the gap as the booking door opens.

As for the people mentioned in this book who helped get the airline off the ground, some have taken up senior positions at low-cost and legacy carriers around the world. Others have left the aviation industry behind, capitalising on the gilt-edged reputation of their former employer. As the airline continues to go from strength to strength there has been no shortage of eager and able candidates to replace them.

The intervening years have for the most part been kind to easyJet. The brand has become a household name for tens of millions across Europe, testimony to the potential of open borders and the free market. The full impact of Brexit has yet to be felt, but with the improved fuel economy of new generation aircraft, the continent's boundaries are no longer a constraint to the expansionist ambitions of route planners. As airlines reap the benefits of enhanced fuel efficiency, faraway cities such as Moscow, Tel Aviv and Marrakech now feature as outlying dots on an ever-expanding speckled orange route map. It is a stark contrast with the three-route network operated by a tiddler of an airline shuttling between Luton and Scotland.

But......have you noticed how there's always a 'but'? Every success story seems to come with a 'but'. There are few if any exceptions. The higher the pinnacle achieved, the greater the distance to fall. Might easyJet one day end up on that long list of once successful and respected, now defunct airlines alongside *Pan Am*, *Laker* and *Swissair*? Constant vigilance against complacency reduces the risk and I consider the airline to be well equipped to deal with the commercial challenges that lie ahead. But the future holds bigger threats than the rough and tumble of free market competition. Some risks are unknown to us today but one stands out above all others. Existential in nature it casts a growing shadow over easyJet, Ryanair and every other airline on the planet. I'm talking of course about climate change and in particular of the impact of aircraft emissions on our environment. Whether the aviation industry faces up to this challenge of its own accord or ends up having change forced upon it by governments, regulators and the wider public it serves, is unclear. But change will come.

The airline's future is for others to shape. My account ends with a final nod to its past, to the origins of easyJet. They were the best of times, and I count myself fortunate to have been there. Those rollercoaster early years when the *easy* brand was built and the foundations of long-term success were laid down. If this book achieves just one thing, I hope it is to demonstrate how a team of unremarkable people with the right motivation, the right leadership and a substantial dose of good fortune, can accomplish the seemingly impossible.

Printed in Great Britain
by Amazon

38043344R00131